THIRTY FRAMES PER SECOND THE VISIONARY ART OF THE MUSIC VIDEO

THIRTY FRAMES PER SECOND   THE VISIONARY ART OF THE MUSIC VIDEO

BY   STEVE REISS &
                                                 NEIL FEINEMAN

PREFACE: A CONVERSATION WITH   MICHAEL STIPE
FOREWORD   JEFF AYEROFF

                                                 HARRY N. ABRAMS, INC.,
                                                 PUBLISHERS

Editor: Elisa Urbanelli
Design: Tolleson Design, San Francisco

Library of Congress Cataloging-in-Publication Data

Reiss, Steven, 1958–
Thirty frames per second : the visionary art of the music video / Steven Reiss and
and Neil Feineman ; preface by Michael Stipe ; foreword by Jeff Ayeroff.
    p. cm.
Includes bibliographical references (p.), videographies, and index.
ISBN 0-8109-4357-3
    1. Music videos—History and criticism. 2. Music videos—Production and
direction. I. Title: Thirty frames per second. II. Feineman, Neil. III. Title.

PN1992.8.M87 R45 2000
780'.26'7—dc21   00-26629

Published in 2000 by Harry N. Abrams, Incorporated, New York

Printed and bound in Japan

Harry N. Abrams, Inc.
100 Fifth Avenue
New York, N.Y. 10011
www.abramsbooks.com

job#.

TABLE OF CONTENTS

PREFACE: A CONVERSATION WITH MICHAEL STIPE

NEIL FEINEMAN

n.f., R.E.M. is a band that has always made videos that were artistic statements, rather than simply promotional vehicles. Why?

m.s., That's easy. The norm was embarrassing and cheesy. It's simple. Each of us felt that videos should be more than visual interpretations of a song. They create narrative and visual landscapes that are different from the way a listener would see music. We didn't want to steal that away from a listener. Instead, we wanted something that would be interesting to people.

n.f., How would you choose the directors?

m.s., For the most part, we chose people who we respected and were capable of good work. I would sit with Randy Skinner [Senior Vice President of Video, Warner Bros. Records] looking at director's reels or be watching television and take notice of a director's work.

n.f., You have a reputation for being surprisingly hands-off

STEPHANE SEDNAOUI:
R.E.M.
LOTUS
1998

with the videos. Do you give the directors total license, or do you look at the director's treatments?

m.s., We certainly look at treatments. It's our money and our time. I didn't want to end up being a human representation of a goldfish, dancing around in a fishbowl.

n.f., Peter Care has said that you actually get the best out of a director because you give them respect.

m.s., Peter has this ability to take a simple idea and then use his bag of tricks to come up with layers and sensibilities. I would say something like "let's do a walking video through the desert" and then I would add "oh, yeah, maybe throw in Andy Kaufman," and Peter would come up with "Man on the Moon." It's a good example of how a director finds ways to bring the band or the performance or an extra character into the video.

n.f., Since you are also involved in features, how are movies and videos different from each other?

m.s., Videos take three days to shoot and cost a lot less money.

n.f., What about the artistic differences?

m.s., I wouldn't want to comment on that. Videos have certainly carved out a niche. And they've created a lot of jobs, and a place for punk rockers to go. It's led them to commercials and films.

n.f., I guess the real question is, do you think music videos are an art form?

m.s., Yeah, No. Okay — I'll give it that, haltingly. Some videos are brilliant emotional or visual creations and do kind of great things. And they've turned around and influenced other mediums, and have had their conventions co-opted by feature films and commercials, and have expanded the idea of narrative.

n.f., When you hear a song, does it make you think of the video?

m.s., It depends. Hopefully, no. The ideal would be that by watching TV or this stunning visual, I'll go back to listening to the song, and that the video doesn't add up to so much that it takes away from the song. But that's really hard to do. So the medium as an art form — those aren't my words, but I guess I do think so. Sure.

They are at least very cool commercials. I do think that now video has fairly exhausted itself. It has developed a language that has been burned into the ground.

In "It's the End of the World As We Know It and I Feel Fine," I wanted to give Jim Herbert free reign. I bought him a book with a picture of a young boy holding a photograph. My idea was to put a tripod in the middle of a creek here in Georgia in high summer, and place the camera so it was shooting upstream, and just run the film for three and a half minutes on this placid setting. It may have been too easy, but I liked the idea of having a frenetic song playing against this image that was like an aquarium. [Then] it was transformed — first it was why not a young guy holding the photo. Then the stream got lost. Then it was a boy with a dog. Then it was a barn. And that was how it went. But I still like the idea of that beautiful, simple image.

n.f., [A brief discussion about the electronic music scene's anti-celebrity posture and the increasing boredom younger people seem to have with celebrity touches on the potential irrelevance of celebrity-driven conventions, such as the music video.] As a celebrity, do you think this disinterest by the general public is good?

m.s., As a celebrity who is actually celebrated for something I do, I welcome it. I have to say that it doesn't take a whole lot to be a celebrity these days — you can have your penis cut off by your wife, or mow your family down with a machine gun, or get caught with your pants down on Wall Street, and the media will do its job and then it's up to you to make the most of it. That cheapens celebrity, so I applaud the idea that people aren't as interested in that anymore. It smacks of artificiality, and they know that.

Visually where do we go from here? We're opening a can of worms, but I wonder what celebrity and the cult of celebrity and advertising will be like in twenty years. There's already so much that's crass and stupid now, but what are people twenty years from now going to think about people just standing there and singing their songs? I don't know if it's going to be enough.

n.f., Maybe your original idea for "It's the End of the World" isn't so far off.

m.s., Yes. An aquarium. It would be nice to look at.

FOREWORD

ROCK 'N' ROLL CHANGED THE WORLD: VIDEO CHANGED ROCK 'N' ROLL

JEFF AYEROFF

Is music video an art form? I think that discussion dates back to the Buggles' "Video Killed the Radio Star." Music video may have destroyed the "purity" of the listening experience, but it created a new model and an earth shatteringly visual one.

There is also no doubt in my mind that many music videos play to the most base elements of our culture. But there are also many videos that show the best elements, and those can only be described as high art.

Those were certainly the standards we tried to hold ourselves up to when we started making these short films. They were meant to be interpretations of a song, and they were meant to be art. You can be a Luddite and hold onto the past and say how great it was before there was video, or you can recognize the beauty and innovation that have come from the world of music video.

The changes that music video have made are pervasive. It has changed advertising. It has changed filmmaking; and it has educated an entire cadre of new creative people who have made their way into the old and new media through music video. Video has changed the nature of how we sell things: whether it's a Buick or a Mountain Dew commercial or a music video itself, the "sell" has become more competitive, more sophisticated, and more interesting. Just ask the people at Coca-Cola, Calvin Klein, and Time-Warner-EMI-AOL.

In 2000, the director Spike Jonze won the MTV Best Director award and was also nominated for an Academy Award for best director for his feature film debut, *Being John Malkovich*. This is big stuff. It means that the music video medium has become a legitimate art form, and that a "farm team," with stars of its own, has brought directors and stylists and choreographers from all over the globe into the broader worlds of entertainment media.

You can talk about this video or that but, at the end of the day, videos such as Mondino's "Boys of Summer," Godley and Creme's "Every Breath You Take," Steve Barron's "Money for Nothing," David Fincher's oeuvre, Michel Gondry's videos for Björk such as "Human Behavior," and Mark Romanek's "Are You Gonna Go My Way?" — to mention just a few — prove that there is no higher form of contemporary "commercial art."

I've been fortunate enough to take musical artists — one must not forget, after all, that without the musician, the medium wouldn't exist — and put them together with visual artists and sit as they discuss what piece of art they can make together. The result is the ultimate collaborative art, music videos. This book shows proof of that collaboration, in all its beautiful, provocative, sensual grandeur.

There will always be a new "idea" in video because that is exactly what video is about: constant reinvention. For now, the images in this book and the videos they represent have changed the world. They haven't necessarily changed it for better or for worse. But they have changed the world — and that's saying something.

edit.

ACKNOWLEDGMENTS

start.

Thirty Frames Per Second is the culmination of more than four years of work and research into the creative process behind the making of the music video.

Although frequently construed as merely a commercial mode to sell records, the videos are a treasure trove rich with provocative imagery, symbolic and metaphorical content, color, texture, and vision. We did not set out to prove any points other than the music video, which is as much about experimental filmmaking as it is about commercial considerations, has in fact made an indelible stamp on popular culture; and that many directors who have indulged in this genre have put forth a body of work which should be recognized, studied, and eventually honored as an art form.

As with every endeavor of this magnitude, it is difficult to include or thank everyone who has made a contribution to this medium, especially when page count is limited and resources are so vast. But we have tried to do our best at delivering a solid cross-section of music videos and directors that stand out among the distinguished field of exceptional work.

We wish to thank the following people for tirelessly helping us during various stages of the production of this book:

thanks.

Rebecca Skinner, Ericka Danko, Emily Koch [HSI]; Scott Flor, Laurie Malaga, Isaac Rice, John Dorsey, Tony Maxwell, Tim Johnson, Grace Upshaw, Topher Dow, and the guys in the vault [Propaganda Films]; Clare Crespo, Janet Haase, Robyn Breen, John T. Dorsey, Howard Shur, Palli Grimsson, Nissar Modi, Micah McKinney [Satellite Films]; Heidi Herzon and Melinda Valente [Oil Factory Inc.]; Nicola Doring [True Comics]; Nick Morris, Jonathan Owen [Academy]; Theresa Boyd [@Radical Media]; Lourri Hammack [Blashfield & Associates]; Bruce Mellon [Original Pictures]; Yamani Watkins [A Band Apart]; Nancy Hacohen [Paradise]; Ellen Dux, Tom Gorai, Jason Free [Pellington-Gorai]; Suzanne Morris, Cora Pyles [Strato]; William Green, Elizabeth Gallagher [The End]; Karla Staab, Jessica Ballard [Gigantic]; Janet Eisner [The A&R Group]; Mary Saxon [Coppos]; TK Knowles [BOB]; Amanda Willgrave, Lisa Bryer [Cowboy]; Holly Ross, Chris Sheffield, Lanette Phillips, Gail Salmo [Palomar]; Marie Perry [Stiefel & Co.]; Charlie Cocuzza [Epoch Films]; Phil Klemmer, James MacKay [Partizan]; Tamara Kaye [Serious Pictures]; Jason Valen, Eric Reed [1171]; David Naylor, Missy Galanida, Emily Skinner, Ned Brown [DNA]; Richard Bell [State]; Hervé Humbert [Bandit]; Ellen Jacobson, Vicki Mayer, Pilar Demnn [Black Dog RSA]; Kelly Norris [Revolver Film Co.]; Rhea Rupert, Janice Biggs [Little Minx]; Lance Anderson, Mark McKenna, Kelley Evans, Jennifer Dynof [Ritts/Hayden]; James Chads [Maguffin]; Alison Riddell [Straw Dogs]; Stefan Sonnenfeld, Missy Papageorge [C03]; Kirsten Andersen, Eileen Dreger, Ruth LeFaive, Amy McArthur, Debbie Richman, Daniel Becerra, Kevin Cloepfil, Robert Dahlin, Patti Gannon, Steve Kokor, Steve Langius, Richard Lieu, Eric Monney, Eric Novisedlak, Jay Odom, Alex Romano, Debra Goodman [525 Studios]; Sue Troyon, Alex Frisch, Scott McNeil, Russ Fell, Don Henry, Chris Staves, Daniel Benoit, Joe Morrison, Mike Coulter, Shannon Marshall [Method]; Joe Matza, David Hays, Carrie Holecek, Patti Mauck, Kit Young, Mark Sachse, Edith Viramontes [Efilm]; Rex Sforza, Leanne Lajoie, Michael Renniger and the art dept., Keith Milton, Amy Stanton and the music video dept., and the Nancy Berry Team [Virgin Records]; Eric LaBrecque, Susan Hootstein, Douglas Gayeton, James Tauber, Tim Clawson, Ben Callet, Seena, Dana & Stacy, Mandy Ingber, Leigh Shelley, Doc Bailey, Andy Slater, Caresse Norman, Craig Fruin, Ross Rosen, Shauna O'Brien, Karen Langford, Tammy Wells, Joseph Penachio, Henry Wrenn-Meleck, Steve Gordon, Alex Springer. Scott Spanjich, Kate Miller, Danny Lockwood, Peter Baron, David Snow, Gina Harrell, Sonia Ives, Lydia and Devin Sarno, Camille Yorrick. And David Reiss for his never ending support from above.

Special thanks to our major sponsor companies:

Virgin Records, 525 Studios, Efilm, Iomega, Method, Loeb & Loeb, Nash Editions

And eternal thanks to the core group of people, who unselfishly gave of their time and resources:

Danielle Cagaanan, a close and dear compatriot in the business who helped us gain momentum and keep the focus — she rocks.

Randy Skinner, one of the most revered persons in the industry, for >>

lending her insight and her experience in the music video world.

Pauline Babikian, for providing what we needed without delay with a smile that could be seen over the phone.

Len Peltier and the people at Virgin Records, especially the art department, for tolerating our many hours on the computers and color printers and hanging around their desks.

Steve Hendricks and Eric Bonniot at 525 Studios. If these angels come to your door, you know you are truly blessed. No facility has supported the music video more in every way, shape, and form.

Doug Faust, for still being a bro', and all the folks at *Revolution*, for putting up with the clutter and distractions.

Jerry Cancellieri and Steve Michaels at Method, for their continued support and good-spirited involvement, not only in this book, but in all the projects that cross their threshold.

Neysa Horsburgh at Method, a true friend and the most stylish person one could know. In one word, royalty.

Mark Romanek, the director and Ashley Beck, the visual effects artist whose work inspired this book and who openly supported the project with faith and wisdom.

Alan Nevins and Joel Gotler at AMG/Renaissance for taking on this project, giving it the utmost respect and attention, and bringing it to the cream of the crop of publishers.

Beth Broday, for having confidence in the project and taking it to Joel and Alan. We will be forever grateful and inspired by her thoughtfulness.

Craig Emanuel and Miles Mogulescu at Loeb & Loeb, for watching our back and giving such sound advice.

Michael Stipe, Meredith Williams, Bertis Downs, and the R.E.M. office, for coming through in the clutch. Special kudos to Michael for his inspired words, soulful music, and videos that transcend time.

Shirley Manson and Matthew Rolston, for allowing us to get intimate with one of their creative correspondences.

Efilm and Joe Matza, for making our final images look so good and putting up with several years of experimenting until we got it right.

Iomega and Joe Bartenhagen, for backing us all the way with Jaz discs.

Mac Holbert and Graham Nash of Nash Editions, for placing the presentation images in their best, most artistic light.

Danny Kaplan, a creative partner during many stages of the book, whose support, encouragement, and design sense helped keep the project on track.

MVPA, and especially Justine Smith, Shana Betz, and Andrea Clark, for helping us get the word out and finding otherwise inaccessible material.

Rock the Vote and Mario Velasquez, for including us in their pilgrimage to raise voter awareness and help make a difference in this country and the world.

Our parade of assistants: Heather Hach, Arianne Autaubo, Michelle Parker, and Willow Tomkins. Their hard work was tremendously appreciated.

All the directors, producers, production companies, record labels, assistants, d.p.s, production designers, stylists, crew members, editors, telecine colorists, visual effects artists, agents, managers, and lawyers who make these little films a reality.

The bands themselves, for making the music that sparks the images in the first place. The world would not be the same without you.

Steve Tolleson, whose design sense, integrity, and style is unequaled, and his hard-working, always pleasant staff who saved the day, everyday, when we thought all was lost. Ellen Elfering, our liaison to that staff and a truly elegant professional. Craig Clark, a forward-thinking designer and person who jammed! René Rosso for burning many candles at many ends, and keeping us organized with quality and aplomb. Sarah White, the ever-calming gatekeeper who let us in even when the door was sometimes locked.

Elisa Urbanelli, our editor and voice to the world. Without Elisa and her belief in us every step of the way, *Thirty Frames Per Second* would not be of sound mind and body. Your name belongs next to ours on the book jacket.

And especially to the generosity of two true giants in the music industry:

Jeff Ayeroff, who was there in the beginning and throughout; who gave immeasurably of his time and contacts; and who has done more for music video than even he realizes.

Nancy Berry, for getting it so quickly, throwing all her resources behind this book, and giving us that rarest of opportunities: "true creative and financial freedom with a nice place to work."

>> **STEVE REISS & NEIL FEINEMAN**

THIRTY FRAMES PER SECOND

THE VISIONARY ART OF THE MUSIC VIDEO

INTRODUCTION

>> No art form is as schizophrenic as the music video. In part a commercial and in part a short film, it has flaunted the line between art and commerce, undermined narrative and character development, and shortened an entire generation's attention span. In the process, it has given new meaning to the term *postmodern,* and has brought the long-simmering debate on the artistic merit of mass media such as movies, photography, television, and graphic design to a fever pitch.

The arguments have not really changed since the early days of MTV. As Michael Shore wrote in *The Rolling Stone Book of Rock Video* way back in 1984, music video is "a bastard offspring of art, falling somewhere between the mini-movie and the maxi-commercial." It is precisely this desire and need to entertain and sell simultaneously, he continues, that creates the great divide between its popular appeal and its ever vocal critics.

On one side are the avant-garde guardians of high culture, who disdain anything that smacks of mainstream appeal. On the other side are, among others, the more proletariat pop and postmodern advocates, whose art is akin to visual sampling.

"Popular culture," explained Lawrence Alloway, in "The Birth of Pop Art," the pop art movement's manifesto of the mid-1950s, "is a vernacular culture that persisted beyond any specific intellectual skills in art, architecture, design, or art criticism. . . . The area of contact was mass-produced urban culture: movies, advertisement, science fiction, Pop music. We felt none of the dislike of common culture standard among most intellectuals but accepted it as fact, discussed it in detail and consumed it enthusiastically."

Unlike the avant-garde, who "used art to dig the trench between art and life, pop did things the other way around — it amalgamated industrial and cultural production by abandoning any idea of educating the public," continued heir apparent Charles Jencks in his book

Post-Modernism. As "the creative reaffirmation of the realities of mass production," pop made a "fetish of the new" and ushered in a fascination with consumer goods as art and the gleeful appropriation (or, as critics would say, plundering) of any image, past or present, that artists could get their hands on.

As befitting proponents of a mass art form, the pop and postmodernist camps also believe there is an inherent social and political cast to their art. Rather than exist in a cultural vacuum, wrote Ihab Hassan in postmodernism's call-to-arms, "POSTmodernISM: A Paracritical Bibliography," "Post-Modernism is essentially subversive in form and anarchic in cultural spirit. It dramatizes its lack of faith in art even as it produces new works of art intended to hasten both cultural and artistic dissolution." In a companion essay, novelist John Barth described post-modern literature: "[It] must be democratic, accessible and able to be reread [with enjoyment]."

POP AND ROCK MUSIC HAS NEVER BEEN FREE FROM VISUAL INPUT.

Although both essays were written before music video began its assault on popular culture, they could well have been talking specifically about it. Indeed, words such as "subversive," "anarchic," "dissolution," and "democratic" go a long way in explaining both the art form and the avant-garde's virulent reaction to it.

It also helps explain why artistic legitimacy has eluded the video genre for so long. As Jim Farber put it in *Rolling Stone* in 1991, "Serious music followers would sooner declare concert T-shirts an aesthetic experience. [The reason critics hate music video is because] video does indeed boldface the connection between music, marketing and image. Gleefully it sells the surface, forcing us to rehear the music through a maze of information relating to fashion, beauty, gossip, persona — things dissenters have long seen as distractions from the 'pure' experience of music."

By invoking the purity of the music, these dissenters enjoy an enviable position. They get to argue substance over style and pound their chests with a higher sense of purpose. They, after all, do not need visuals to hear the music.

At least in theory. But the theory is flawed on at least two counts. First, pop and rock music have never really been free from visual input. Whether it was Bill Haley rocking around the clock, Little Richard tutting his frutti, or Elvis gyrating his hips, the music business has never been shy about selling itself. In addition, it has never underestimated the importance of image, or been afraid of enlisting fashion, magazines, film, television, and, in Farber's words, a "subconscious whirl of sources" to help the fan hear the music (and buy the record/8-track/CD).

In this far more accurate light, music video is just the latest in the music biz's parade of visual aids. Undoubtedly, it is also one of the most efficient. Unlike operettas, musicals, or feature-length films, for instance, the video gets right down to business — no extraneous narrative, characters, or words. It "just" sells the performer and the music, not to mention the director, the cinematographer, the set designer, and the stylist.

But the sell is much more difficult than it looks. It is unlike that of a commercial, which only has to sell a tangible product in less than a minute, or of a movie, which has two hours to meander. Instead, the video exists in a previously uncharted three-minute netherworld, and it is selling something far more elusive than a deodorant, a car, or a can of soda.

As a result, the video has to be densely textured so it can hold up over repeated viewings. It has to be edgy enough to be noticed, but palatable enough to satisfy the often divergent demands of the performer, the record company, and the public (a.k.a. the lowest common denominator).

NOTHING COMPARES TO U

^ SINEAD O'CONNOR

1990

v SHARA NELSON

DOWN THAT ROAD

1993

JOHN MAYBURY

With that sort of imperative, some of music video's most derided "failings" become understandable, if not downright virtuous. Although it is commonly attacked for destroying narrative, for example, a plot-driven video usually gets boring the third time you watch it and unbearable soon thereafter. Knowing that their videos are meant to be seen repeatedly, most video directors therefore prefer a denser, more abstract style to telling a simple, literal story.

Similarly, the emphasis on emotion, rather than on analytical character development or ideas, can be seen as the distillation of an age-old impulse to use music as the filmmaker's cornerstone or point of departure. It is no surprise that the first sound film was a musical, *The Jazz Singer*. What may be surprising, however, is that several years later studios such as Paramount were setting the stage for the modern music video with short musical films.

Imaginatively called "short films," these three-to-eight-minute mini-features showcased singers such as Bessie Smith, Billie Holliday, Duke Ellington, Cab Calloway, and Bing Crosby. (Yes. Bing.) Sandwiched between the coming attractions, the newsreel, the serial, the cartoons, and, on Tuesday, the Fiestaware giveaway, these films were commissioned for the simple reason that the theater owners needed filler to get patrons in the door.

Like the videos that were to follow, these short films belied their pragmatic origins by being much, much better than they needed to be. Because they were under less scrutiny by the censorship boards than feature-length films, the short films were often more daring and more cynical than the movies they supported. Anticipating a trend that would continue to mark the form for years, most were simple performances done on a sound stage or a set. The more ambitious ones, however, were mini-narratives laced with irony, socioeconomic reality, and political depth.

Cab Calloway's "Jitterbug Party," for instance, used cinematic devices, including the performance within a performance and breaking the fourth wall, that anticipated modern music video by decades, and pointedly used the musicians to make scathing social and political comments. The film begins with a gussied up Cab performing before an all-white audience in one of Harlem's fancier clubs. The performance seems slightly off kilter. The reason becomes readily apparent once Cab and his band go offstage and, with the camera rolling, slip out on a tour of the "real" Harlem. As the places he brings us to become more authentic, his performance becomes less mannered and far more impassioned.

Although these short films have obvious historical and cultural value today, they were seen as fodder then, so only a handful of them survive. Similarly, only remnants and rumors remain of more experimental musical shorts that were shot in Europe. Of these, the best known were made by the German filmmaker Oskar Fischinger. His films, which used abstract images that were tightly synchronized to classical music and jazz, were successful enough to bring him to America. His best-known work is the opening sequence in *Fantasia*, which in turn is widely considered as an important influence on the modern music video.

ALTHOUGH THE SHORT FILMS HAVE OBVIOUS *HISTORICAL VALUE, THEY WERE SEEN* THEN AS FODDER.

>> "Every once in awhile, a director comes a long that really appreciates how free the medium of music videos can be. Maybe no one's paying attention, or maybe the label and band are trusting and open-minded. That rare situation is when those videos get made that make your brain bend."

— *CLARE CRESPO, FORMER EXECUTIVE PRODUCER OF SATELLITE FILMS*

edit.

>> "Video has really been a mirror for music. It has reflected and, more importantly, has influenced and led culture. We liked to think that we were making little artful music films when I started out. MTV pretty much accepted almost anything back in the day so we didn't feel the pressure as much. Now, there is an extreme amount of pressure. Videos often seem more difficult to make. I still really love the creative process of making them; but, the stakes can sometimes make for a love/hate relationship."

— *SONIA IVES, VICE PRESIDENT CREATIVE SERVICES - ISLAND DEF JAM*

By World War II, changing viewing patterns and needs had eliminated the theatrical demand for the short musical film. After the war, though, the form resurfaced, this time as programming for a cumbersome video jukebox called the Panarom Sound. Each Sound weighed two tons and had a twenty-inch diagonal screen and rear projection film system. Despite its weight, the Sound became a fixture in juke joints and bars across the country, showcasing a wide variety of pop, jazz, and r&b performers, most probably in performance-oriented films. By the early 1950s, television and the machine's weight had made the Sound obsolete. Like the short films of the 1930s, the films themselves disappeared with the machines.

(The video jukebox had a brief resurrection in the 1960s in Europe. Called the French Scopitone, it featured conceptual, color 16 mm music films with French, European, or international hits such as Petula Clark's "Downtown," Dionne Warwick's "Walk on By," and Neil Sedaka's "Calendar Girl," directed by new kids on the block such as Claude Lelouch.)

Unfortunately, we have also lost countless musical "videos" made for early television shows such as *Your Hit Parade* and the less-remembered *It's Happening Baby*. According to scholars of the era, these films accompanied cover versions of the songs, rather than recordings of the original performers. Without access to the stars, a filmed performance was deemed less impressive than a vignette that toyed with literal visual representations of the lyrics or even with fragments of narrative.

The short film also found a home in, of all places, the original *American Bandstand*. This show was not hosted, as is popularly believed, by Dick Clark, but by a man named Bob Horn. And the show did not feature kids dancing to 45 r.p.m.s, but rather to musical short films, which Horn called "Snaders," after their director, George Snader. Amazingly, the show lasted a year before its producers decided that the videos were less interesting and more troublesome than shots of kids dancing to the songs. The *Bandstand* kids were great, but, *Hairspray* notwithstanding, you cannot begin to imagine what pop culture would have been like had the powers that were decided to stick with the videos.

No matter. By then, the action had shifted to occasional guest performances on variety shows and, more lavishly, onto the big screen. The 1956 drama, *Blackboard Jungle*, was the first film credited with using rock music as shorthand for teenage rebellion, and it spawned a genre of mostly terrible movies called "jukebox musicals." Inadvertently, it also provided the first instance of a movie's ability to sell a song. Its theme song, "Rock Around the Clock," had been a modest hit when it had been released the year before. The movie not only resurrected it, but also gave it the exposure it needed to become a classic.

THE SHORT FILM FOUND A HOME IN, OF ALL PLACES, THE ORIGINAL AMERICAN BANDSTAND.

Because only a few of these films, most notably *Jailhouse Rock* and *The Girl Can't Help It,* transcended the limitations of the genre, they are rarely mentioned as having any influence on today's music video. Still, the oft-seen "Jailhouse Rock" number and clips such as Little Richard from *The Girl Can't Help It,* along with famous television set pieces of that era — such as Elvis's *Ed Sullivan* performances — have had an undeniable influence on the form.

The English invasion of the mid-1960s gave music video its next jump-start. English television had already discovered the viability of rock, with its popular shows, *Top of the Pops* and *Ready, Steady, Go.* The latter spun off an American version, called *Shindig,* which in turn spawned a Yank competitor called *Hullaballoo.*

These shows needed musical acts, and needed them every week. The only problem was that international travel was costly and complicated. To make life easier and cheaper, the record companies started financing short promotional films of their more important bands. These films usually relied on concert footage, but occasionally strayed from that format. Because they satisfied the demand for visual context, these promo films quickly became viable alternatives to touring, making them fixtures on the rock-oriented television shows.

As the bands became more popular, the films became more extravagant. By all accounts, some of these films were extraordinary. Since memory loss was an occupational hazard of the 1960s, details, including who directed the piece or even whether or not it was completed, often are hazy. Nevertheless, some landmarks remain.

"We Can Work It Out," "Paperback Writer," and later, "Penny Lane," "Strawberry Fields Forever," and "Hey Jude," for instance, signaled the Beatles' shift from a touring band to recording artists. Others, such as the

Kinks' "Dead End Street," the Who's "Happy Jack" (available on the long-form video, *The Kids Are Alright*), and the Rolling Stones' collaborations with Michael Lindsay-Hogg on the psychedelic "Child of the Moon" and the drag fantasy "Have You Seen Your Mother, Baby, Standing in the Shadow," remain classics of the genre, as well as valuable precursors of the modern music video.

For the most part, at least among American audiences, these promo films are more talked about than seen. Today's video makers were far more likely exposed to pop-influenced television shows like *Batman* or *The Monkees.* The Prefab Four deserve special consideration, since they were among the first to be chosen more for how they would play on TV than for how they would sound on radio. With a support system that included songwriters Neil Diamond and Boyce and Hart, as well as director Bob Rafelson, this show introduced future video directors to a surrealistic, lowbrow, and accessible mix of action, jump cuts, and music that anticipated rock video by a good fifteen years.

If you did not have a television, no worries. You could see many of the same devices at your local theater. As Rafelson was to complain much later, most of the devices normally attributed to the music video, including nonlinear storytelling, speed-of-sound editing, and the elevation of style over character development, were staples of 1960s film. Films such as *Easy Rider, The Thomas Crown Affair, Bonnie and Clyde, M.A.S.H., The Graduate, Blow-Up, Zabriskie Point, 2001, Performance, Woodstock,* and *A Clockwork Orange,* not to mention virtually dialogue-free films such as *Point Blank* and the Clint Eastwood/Sergio Leone spaghetti westerns, were impressing young filmgoers with a new visual sensibility.

"Almost all the effects you see in video today, the psychedelic solarization, the quick cutting, are things we

"ALMOST ALL THE EFFECTS YOU SEE IN VIDEO TODAY, THE PSYCHEDELIC SOLARIZATION, THE QUICK CUTTING, ARE THINGS WE WERE DOING YEARS AGO."

— BOB RAFELSON

were doing years ago. It's really hard to imagine that video directors who are using these special effects really think they are doing anything new," Rafelson said. Although a notoriously bitter man, his comments are validated by watching Rafelson's own *Head* and its immediate precursors, *A Hard Day's Night* and *Help*. All three have more jump cuts, people playing themselves, and cinema verité per minute than the most frenetic music video.

NO ONE, INCLUDING QUEEN, *WAS PREPARED FOR THE SUCCESS OF THE VIDEO FOR* **"BOHEMIAN RHAPSODY."**

The potential for sound on film was not lost on astute musical artists such as Captain Beefheart. Somehow Beefheart convinced Warner Bros. to finance a sixty-second television commercial for *Lick My Decals Off, Baby*. No one had tried to construct an actual television ad campaign for an album before, so Warner Bros. had no system of control in place. To the band and label's disappointment, timid programmers deemed the finished work too strong for commercial broadcast. Still, it made the rounds of industry screenings, attracted a critical buzz, and ultimately was included in the Museum of Modern Art's initial collection of videos.

While the video did not sell Beefheart's albums, it helped push the concept of the promotional film to the next level. America had discovered that teenagers are the ultimate consumers; and no one was in a better position to exploit this market than the record companies. To capitalize on the youth explosion, the companies were signing more bands than they could possibly handle. Suddenly a label had up to fifty bands to showcase and promote. Unless the company was willing to stage a mini-Woodstock for its sales and marketing force, they had no way to introduce them internally to the people who were supposedly making them successful.

Once more, the promo film proved its worth. Rather than bring the bands to the conventions, the label employees could now watch them on the screen. Then, after they had been brought up to speed, the films could be shipped to outposts such as Australia, where the media-starved youth could see and hear what the bands sounded like.

By the mid-1970s, these films were an integral part of teens' rock experience. Their success, coupled with the success promoters such as Don Kirschner and Lorne Michaels were having in America with late-night rock, prompted a producer named Jo Bergman to pitch a video TV show to the networks in 1975. They quickly passed. TV, they told her, had inferior sound quality; and American teenagers didn't stay home at night to watch TV. "Rock," they categorically concluded, "doesn't play on TV."

It's not just hindsight that proved them wrong. A year earlier, England had already demonstrated the power of video with Queen's 1974 masterpiece, "Bohemian Rhapsody." Granted, England was not America, with its more compact, more accessible, and — thanks to the use of film clips of bands on *Top of the Pops* and *Ready, Steady, Go* — more visually literate audience. Still, nothing had prepared anyone, including Queen, for the success of the video of "Bohemian Rhapsody."

The song had posed problems from the outset, primarily because it was so textured that it was virtually impossible to play live. As a compromise, the band decided to shoot a video to support it. It was directed by Bruce Gowers in four hours for seven thousand dollars, and was shown for the first time on *Top of the Pops* several weeks after the single had been released. By the time the

>> "MTV has accelerated the process by which people are more likely to think in images than in logic."

— TODD GITLIN, PROFESSOR OF SOCIOLOGY, UNIVERSITY OF CALIFORNIA AT BERKELEY

KEVIN GODLEY & LOL CREME   >>

<<   *PAULA GREIF & PETER KAGAN*

(I JUST) DIED IN YOUR ARMS TONIGHT
CUTTING CREW
1986

EVERY BREATH YOU TAKE
THE POLICE
1983

video was shown, the song looked like it would be a well-reviewed minor hit, and nothing more. Confounding everyone, the video propelled the song straight to number one. More impressively, fueled by what then passed for heavy rotation, the video kept it there for eleven weeks. Anyone who was paying attention now knew that, under the right circumstances, video could not just support a song. It could make it a hit.

That lesson was not lost on the industry, but still it took five years for someone to actually collect the videos under one umbrella. It is fitting that the credit for the first weekly video show, called *The Kenny Everett Video Show,* which premiered on English television in 1979, belongs in part to David Mallet. Virtually encapsulating the past, present, and future of music video, Mallet had cut his teeth on *Ready, Steady, Go* and *Shindig* fifteen years earlier and was about to direct groundbreaking videos for David Bowie.

By then, videos were also making commercial inroads in America. While *American Bandstand* remained disinterested, its principal competitor, *America's Top Ten,* frequently featured rock videos. Music video, said its voice,

ever-tightening AOR (album-oriented rock) format was making it increasingly difficult to break a song. Cable TV, on the other hand, was exploding. Because it needed programming, it eagerly offered the airwaves to the bands, who were symbiotically rewarded with effective, reasonably inexpensive exposure.

Regardless of the motivation behind them, the best videos radiated artistic and creative excitement. David Bowie, already a major international star, was perhaps the first hero to make his mark. Music video, he said, is "the logical fulfillment of art and technological destiny . . . I see it as an artistic extension. I can visualize the day when the interface of music and video will create an entirely new kind of artist."

Bowie's endorsement was not entirely unexpected — he had, after all, been acting rather than singing his songs for years, and had even used Luis Buñuel's *Un Chien Andalou* as his opening act on the Thin White Duke (Station to Station) tour. These videos from the late 1970s and 1980, including the still provocative "Boys Keep Swinging," "Look Back in Anger," "Ashes to Ashes," and "Fashion" (all directed by Mallet), were logical

>> "Making a video is like making love. It's fraught with danger."

– BETTE MIDLER

edit.

Mr. Top 40 himself, Casey Casem, "was the most exciting new art form in the world today." Todd Rundgren agreed. "Rock video is the wave of the future," he declared, shortly before sinking two million dollars into Utopia Video Studios. And an entrepreneur named Ed Steinberg started RockAmerica, a video pool that supplied videos not just to cable TV but to trade shows and rock clubs.

The acceptance, again, had less to do with artistic potential than with marketing considerations. Radio's

extensions of Bowie's persona. They were also convincing arguments for the form's viability.

From a conceptual perspective, the videos from Devo were at least as important as Bowie's because they were conceived with the express purpose of establishing the band's artistic identity and commercial presence. "Devo," says band member Gerry Casale, who worked with Chuck Slater on many of the videos, "was into the idea of making films, or videos, or whatever you want to

WHY STOP AT A VIDEO SHOW, *WHEN YOU COULD HAVE AN ENTIRE NETWORK* **DEVOTED TO** **MUSIC VIDEO?**

call them, not as some promotional afterthought but as an integral part of our overall artistic and marketing approach. To us, it was a very quaint, obsolete, holdover-1960s Uptopian idea to keep the music and marketing separate. This is the music business, and its business is music. You can't separate the two; they're parts of the same whole." In their own way, then, Devo was not just aligned with art-rock bands such as the Talking Heads or Bowie, but with pop-culture constructs like the Monkees.

Devo certainly shared a love of the medium with ex-Monkee Michael Nesmith. Realizing that cable now offered the ability to promote music in stereo, Nesmith was busy producing a show for Nickelodeon called *Popclips,* which was hosted by "V-J" Howie Mandel, It featured videos such as Mallet's "I Don't Like Mondays" for the Boomtown Rats, which was a full-blown concept video complete with multiple sets, characters, and the semblance of a plot, and Russell Mulcahy's prophetic "Video Killed the Radio Star" for the Buggles.

Popclips gave the folks at Warner Cable an idea. Why stop at a video show when you could have an entire network devoted to music video? Why indeed. As the

Music Television, the first major telecommunications medium ever to merge the power of stereophonic sound with the visual impact of TV," its press release read. "MTV is cable's first all-music channel, beamed by satellite in stereo, 24 hours a day. It will show state-of-the-art video records of contemporary artists performing their music. These video records are more than just a tape of a band playing and singing. They are highly stylized visual interpretations of the music, using the most advanced video techniques. And the sound is transmitted through stereo speakers, bringing a whole new dimension to the way people watch TV."

MTV made good on its promise almost immediately, by taking an obscure novelty song, "Mickey," sung and staged by Mallet's former assistant, Toni Basil, to the top of the charts. Because the track's success was inextricably linked to the video and MTV, it is fitting that Basil was the first person to sign a contract as both a music and visual artist.

Basil took the distinction seriously. "My videos represent the culmination of an eighteen-year career," she told an interviewer shortly after "Mickey"'s success.

>>   "I want to turn into a monster."

— MICHAEL JACKSON'S ONE-LINE PITCH TO JON LANDIS FOR "THRILLER"

edit.

Wall Street Journal was fond of reporting, the music business was in the doldrums. No one was moving records, and no one was having any fun. The vision that was to become MTV may have struck some as half-baked; but others, such as television mogul Fred Silverman, got it immediately. "MTV," he announced, "is the most interesting and exciting new thing to happen to television yet." "The biggest advertising venture in history," echoed *Billboard* magazine.

Appropriately, MTV beat its own drum best. "MTV.

"They're all-consuming for me, like monsters that create themselves. I get very compulsive about them. Though everyone says my videos are all about fun, and they basically are, I still see them as art pieces."

It was easy for the MTV machine, which almost immediately included the record companies, to encourage videos as sunny as Basil's. Devo soon found out, however, that less cheerful work would not get played. One of Devo's first videos, a Buñuel-ish homage with disturbingly

STEVE BARRON

BILLIE JEAN
^ MICHAEL JACKSON
                              1983

TAKE ON ME
^   a-ha   1985

>> "One of the first 'music videos' I can remember that steam-rolled my prepubescent mind was some liquid-light, chroma-key Ike & Tina spectacle. It oozed in so many ways. Beautiful, horrifying and pitifully simple. A potent combination that I wish came around to visit more often."

— DEVIN SARNO, SENIOR DIRECTOR, VIDEO PRODUCTION, EPIC RECORDS GROUP

"VIDEO IS AS
CLOSE AS THE
CINEMA HAS COME
TO THE IMPRESSIONISM
OF THE LYRIC POEM."

— FRANK McCONNELL

perverse imagery, prompted A&M to reject the band. "Sorry. You guys are just too bizarre for us. But keep making those great films," the executive said.

The preponderance of all those shiny, happy faces on the television obscured most of the period's most challenging videos, and almost certainly helped make video a cheap target for most critics. Even so, some people, such as Frank McConnell, who lauded video as a significant advance in an article called "Infant Art" in *Commonweal* magazine, championed the form early on.

Video, he wrote, is
a three-minute art form that grew up, like most art forms, accidentally. For originally it was intended simply as a visual adjunct to records about to be marketed by major groups. Its nearest antecedents are, probably, TV commercials . . . or brilliant short bits of filmmaking like the main title sequences of the James Bond or Pink Panther movies.

Short, fast, hallucinatory and lyrical; those are the characteristics of video at its best. And as the form evolves, it is interesting to see how the filmmaking eventually becomes as important as, or more important than, the lyrics of the song itself. . . . [Blending TV and music], it is generating a form which is perhaps as close as the cinema has come to the impressionism of the lyric poem, and as close as rock has approached to the status of symbolism.

Most critics, however, typically treated music video as the end of the world as we knew it. In January 1984, for instance, Joe Saltzman likened music video to brain death in the tellingly titled "Predigested Dreams" in, of all places, the distinctly mainstream *USA Today*.

"They have gone and done it again," he wrote. *They've taken the music to which kids used to read, do their homework, even dream, and have added pictures to it. No longer is it possible to close your eyes and fantasize personal images to "Dancing with Myself," "Safety Dance," or "Don't Forget to Dance." The new music videos have taken care of that. They now provide the pictures for the songs in our heads. Goodbye, imagination.*

A less infuriated writer might have recognized a good exit line when he saw one, but Saltzman was on a roll. *What's worse is that most of the images supplied with the music are as bizarre a grouping as ever created for the moving screen. Even Ken Russell [a British art director famous for his rococo, over-the-top visual flair] might blanch at the violent, sexual, obscure, seemingly random images that go into the majority of these three-minute video packages.*

You could almost see him salivating as he drove the message home:
Before MTV, the song, no matter how silly or pretentious, could be used as a springboard to a range of emotions most teenagers felt. The lyric, the loud beat of the music, could lead to self-created, very personal images being conjured that might help teens give form to vague troubles. Now here comes the music video to destroy all that. They are self-contained packages of sight and sound. All kids have to do is watch and listen and stare straight ahead. No need to think, to embellish, to create, to imagine. The electric fix is in.

Strangely, it never occurred to him or the others that there was a simple solution to the problem, which was to change the channel or turn the TV off. In any event, he was right: The fix was truly in. "Predigested Dreams" notwithstanding, *USA Today* regularly chronicled the latest Michael Jackson or Madonna video with fanfare worthy of a blockbuster studio premiere. A-list directors such as Martin Scorsese, Jon Landis, and Brian de Palma went slumming in the video trough, often with budgets that, minute for minute, matched those of their feature films. The corner bar suddenly had sprouted banks of video monitors. Acts like Duran Duran became superstars largely because of their videos. The Buggles had it right after all.

Ten years later, the song remained pretty much the same. "Do You Still Want Your MTV?" John Leland asked in *Newsweek* in 1994. "Yes," was the resounding answer. "MTV has changed the way we talk, dress, dance, make, and consume music and how we process information. It created a new breed of visual pop star: Cyndi Lauper, Boy George, Janet Jackson and Madonna. And its reach is growing."

The critics, for the most part, were still unconvinced. In an irony that was not lost on Leland, many of them hated video with the same fervor their parents had lavished on rock and roll. "MTV is the rock revolution all over again — alienating the grown-ups, alarming the alarmists, impressing the impressionable to adopt silly hairstyles," he wrote.

Since these adults had been raised on rock themselves, they should have known better. But like their parents, who had been "horrified by Elvis's pelvis in the 1950s," Leland went on, "an older generation worries that MTV will seduce their children with its hypnotic sexuality, though the network rejects explicitly sexual material."

The lack of explicit material, however, could not disguise the stream of sexual imagery. "MTV brings new visual ideas to light faster than any other medium, embracing high art and trash — selections from Kafka

and biker sluts — with equal zest," Leland wrote. "Instead of venting raw libido, it makes all of life a cool sexual fetish. And it pitches those fetishes, along with messages flogging the environment, voter registration, the newest hit record, clothes, and a hip lifestyle — in an undifferentiated mesh of hype."

That hype not only packaged sex, but fashion as well. As Warren Morris, in "The Great Music Video Question," wrote, videos "have taught us to watch as well as listen to pop music. In the process, they've opened vistas on sexual behavior and gender roles previously hidden from public view. The display of androgyny, for one, has become commonplace."

So, he continues, have sadomasochism, merry-widow corsets, French garter belts, fishnet stockings, distressed denim, tattoo transfers, spandex jumpsuits, and phosphorescent hair dye, not to mention Panama hats, monster masks, hi-tech furniture, codpieces, reflector sunglasses, leather bow ties, art-deco lamps, martini glasses, and sequined gloves. "Where did people see them first?" he asks. "Guess."

This unprecedented immediacy has social, economic, and political implications. In addition to influencing style, the videos were a harbinger of the global economy and helped redefine retail. In the past, manufacturers and retailers could take three years to break a look or a line from the coasts to the "flyover" regions. But videos destroyed that luxury. Since everyone saw the videos simultaneously, the clothes and accessories had to be in every mall in every city at once. Some surfwear companies calculated that their window of opportunity suddenly shrank from three years to six weeks.

Strictly speaking, of course, these effects do not make videos art. As critics were quick to point out, videos should be good at selling fashion, trends, and styles, because they are commercials. That is what commercials do.

"MTV HAS CHANGED THE WAY WE TALK, DRESS, DANCE, MAKE, AND CONSUME MUSIC."

— JOHN LELAND

"BLAMING MTV FOR ROTTING
THE AMERICAN MIND
HAS ALWAYS BEEN A
POINTLESS EXCERCISE,
GIVEN TELEVISION'S
TRADITION OF
IMBECILIC
PROGRAMMING."

— MICHAEL HIRSCHORN

Art, they argued, is another story. On that score, videos still fell far short of their mark. The laundry list of their shortcomings started with their bombastic nature and their promotion of sensation and style over genuine emotion and substance. It then moved on to include the impression that videos were derivative, formulaic, juvenile, and egocentric, and ended with the notion that they were, for the most part, unwatchable.

Graham Fuller articulately spelled the situation out in "A Good Music Video Is Hard to Find" (*Interview*, October 1996). "The search for art and artistry of the music videos goes on but the consensus is that El Dorado or Santa Claus will turn up first. . . . Fifteen years after the inception of MTV, what critical evaluation of music video that there is relegates it to the trash can of popular culture."

A well-turned phrase, but one that in the end begs the question. He's right in that it would be foolish to argue that there are more good videos than bad ones. There aren't. Be that as it may, no art form has ever been defined by its ratio of bad to good work. Painting is not. Classical music is not. Literature, theater, and photography are not. So why should music video be judged by that standard?

To quote Douglas Coupland on the subject, "About 90 percent of the videos we see are shaped by formulas so predictable as to render them wallpaper." After revising the figure to 95 percent, he then goes on to say that the remaining "five percent take one back to that first, surging crest of curiosity, excitement, sensuality, and

desirability of all good videos. Let us watch these videos and let us crackle with excitement and burn with color."

The complaints that videos favor short attention spans, value style over substance, and rely on montage rather than on traditional character development and narrative also say less about video than they do about the times. Videos may indeed embody these values, but you could say the same thing about almost everything on the screen and stage, or even about many books, newspapers, and magazines. Attention spans have gotten shorter; and, across the board, entertainment and art have become more sensational. That's just the way it is.

As we have already seen, while video was undoubtedly instrumental in the shift from a traditional literary style, many films and TV shows of the 1960s and 1970s played to those same impulses. So did those pesky surrealists and Dadaists in the early part of the twentieth century, not to mention novelists like Joyce, Dos Passos, Pynchon, and DeLillo. Video may have killed the radio star, but traditional literary sensibility had been on life support for years.

Indeed, as Michael Hirschorn noted in the October 1990 issue of *Esquire*,
Blaming MTV for rotting the American mind has always been a pointless exercise, given television's long tradition of imbecilic programming. Far from representing a decline in standards, MTV in recent years has matured into a rare forum of video creativity and catholicity of taste. The network that once feared to play Michael Jackson [as too black] now

>> "The success of MTV [relies on] the understanding that the channel offers not videos but environment, a context that creates mood. These are fascinating and disturbing elements of a form that becomes not only a way of seeing and hearing but of being. Music videos invent the world they represent."

— *PAT AUFDERHEIDE, CULTURAL EDITOR*, IN THESE TIMES

edit.

>> "Video directors reprove what good film directors knew all along — that visuals can also be music. When executed with élan, an edit becomes a backbeat, a crane shot a solo, a close-up a hook."
— *JIM FARBER, "THE 100 TOP MUSIC VIDEOS," ROLLING STONE, OCTOBER 14, 1993*

edit.

has spurred the rise of rap to musical preeminence and has promoted a wide variety of avant-garde and otherwise obscure musicians. No commercial and few public radio stations can make a similar claim. No television network comes close.

He is right. Although videos may all look alike to the disdainful critic, they come in all sizes, shapes, and colors. There are performance-driven videos, such as Bruce Springsteen's "Dancing in the Dark," Aerosmith and Run D.M.C.'s "Walk This Way," Mick Jagger and Bowie's "Dancing in the Streets," and Lenny Kravitz's "Are You Gonna Go My Way." There are narrative videos such as Michael Jackson's "Beat It" and "Thriller," the Beastie Boys' "Sabotage," Pearl Jam's "Jeremy," and Madonna's "Like a Virgin." There are gothic videos, such as Nine Inch Nails' "Closer," and animated or computer-ized videos, such as Dire Straits' "Money for Nothing," a-ha's "Take On Me," and Peter Gabriel's "Sledgehammer." There are moody dreamscapes like Don Henley's "Boys of Summer" and k.d. lang's "Constant Craving"; classic por-traiture, such as Chris Isaak's "Wicked Games" and Sinead O'Connor's "Nothing Compares 2 U"; futuristic extravaganzas, like Duran Duran's "Wild Boys" and Jackson's "Scream"; and up-close-and-personal home movies, such as Fiona Apple's "Shadowboxer."

The video's ability to handle diverse images, styles, and techniques — often within an individual director's portfolio — has forced us to redefine the concept of the auteur. Traditionally an auteur would be able to tick off a list of signature traits common to his or her work. Robert Altman, for instance, could be recognized for his use of elliptical style, overlapping dialogue, and celebrity cameo appearances.

ALTHOUGH VIDEOS MAY ALL LOOK ALIKE TO THE DISDAINFUL CRITIC, **THEY COME IN ALL SIZES, SHAPES, AND COLORS.**

Music video directors must tailor each video to the song and have far less room to move than they would with a longer, more modulated feature-film script, so they don't have the same luxury of fully developing distinctive visual signatures. But video directors have compensated by becoming extremely good with the time they have. Despite the compressed format, they have managed to stamp their videos with personalized styles, looks, and themes. In the process, they are increasingly treated as true auteurs.

A 1997 article in *Time*, for example, devoted considerable space to an analysis of the work of Floria Sigismondi, Paul Hunter, Hype Williams, and Jonathan Glazer. Others contrast the work of newer talents such as Sigismondi with more established directors such as Matthew Rolston or Mark Romanek in much the same way that film critics compare Quentin Tarantino and the Coen Brothers to Woody Allen and Scorsese. Thus, like the directors' credits that are now included as a matter of course on videos, it is no longer unusual to talk about a director as having a distinctive video style.

This visual control used to stem from the lack of a band's involvement with the video — for the most part, most of the bands are still more interested in music than in acting. This was particularly true in the beginning. Russell Mulcahy, for example, remembers a period in the early 1980s when Virgin "was signing new bands left, right, and center; and I was making at least a promo clip a week for all of them, OMD, XTC, the Members, the Human League, even the Sex Pistols and Public Image Ltd. I was still writing all the concepts; most bands didn't have any input at all. They'd just turn up for the shoot

JIM BLASHFIELD

AND SHE WAS
TALKING HEADS   1985
<<

GOOD FRIENDS
JONI MITCHELL   1985
<<

0:00:25

and say, 'right, what do you want us to do?' It was only occasionally that a band like XTC would take any real strong interest in the concept."

These days, bands may be more involved in the process but still trust the director. As this letter from Shirley Manson of Garbage to Matthew Rolston attests, the director is still at the heart of the process. The subject is "I Think I'm Paranoid."

Dear Matthew:

Hope all is well!
Here is a list of our video comments! Hope that they don't crush your vibe too much as you so totally rocked our world. We absolutely love the way you made us look in it! Even Duke is happy!!! You are a master of your art dahling!!!!!!

Firstly . . . here are a few things we LOVE.
We love when the film is turned into negative.
We love the "With the Beatles" shots.
We love the editing and all the shots in the breakdown middle eight and outro. It looks and feels perfect.
We love the mylar shots of Shirley . . . as they are less fashion oriented and a little more obtuse. They lend a little more mystique to the overall feel of the video.
We don't want the viewer to be completely sickened by her visage by the time the video is shown more than once.
We love the way you have made us all look forty years younger!!! Ha ha hee ho hum . . .

So . . . on to the negative nastiness . . . boo hisssssss . . .
Upon looking at the video several times, we changed our mind about wanting any more "mouth" shots. There seem to be plenty. You were right the first time big boy.

In general we think the video is great but could do with being made a little edgier. We also feel that although the pacing of the editing fits the pacing of the song, we still need for the first minute or so of the video to be ever so slightly more aggressively edited. Just to make it slightly weirder.

We want ALL the boot "stomping" and "kicking" out! It looks like we are trying too hard to be "naughty" or "hard." Except for both the shots of the legs around the line "heaven knows what you've got to prove."

The director is clearly the glue that holds the video together. Graeme Whifler, who directed early, classic videos for the Residents, says it well. "Directing a rock video means you have to be a director, writer, producer, advertising executive, and psychiatrist all at once. Most bands are rather inarticulate with their concepts, and aren't used to acting for the camera. To me, the funny thing about rock video is that they're like silent films: There's no dialogue, just the music and the visuals. It's like the film industry is starting over again from ground zero."

Video directors are now beginning to rewrite the rules of feature films as well, since music video is proving to be an increasingly fertile training ground for features, as witnessed by the success of directors such as Julian Temple, Russell Mulcahy, Michael Bay, David Fincher, Dominic Sena, and Spike Jonze. Some directors, used to the more freewheeling world of music video, with its more single-minded focus the short films permit, have had trouble adapting to the demands of a big-budget Hollywood film.

One highly respected video director, frustrated by having nothing to show for an abortive foray into the studio

> "MOST BANDS WOULD JUST TURN UP **FOR THE SHOOT AND SAY,** 'RIGHT, WHAT DO YOU WANT US TO DO?'"
>
> — RUSSELL MULCAHY

>> "My videos are all-consuming, like monsters that create themselves."

— TONI BASIL

edit.

RATHER THAN DESTROY THE VIEWER'S ABILITY TO INTERPRET THE SONG, MANY DIRECTORS DELIBERATELY DESIGN THE VIDEO TO ELICIT AN OPEN-ENDED RESPONSE.

system, goes so far as to say that the more creative the music video director, the more suited he or she will be in the independent film arena. Other arguably creative directors, such as Mulcahy and Fincher, have performed well for the major studios, and have gone on record describing their video training as ideal preparation for their work in features.

It is easy to see why. With or without band involvement, the demands of the medium — and the emerging tyranny of the remote control — tend to favor a strong director with a coherent vision. "With remote control in hand," wrote Hirschorn in that same *Esquire* piece, "viewers will zap any show that bores them, searching the bowels of their cable system for something, anything, that is entertaining. MTV has learned that it must beat the competition image for image, split second for split second, throughout the day — in this new world, a half hour might as well be a lifetime, and linearity is a truly outmoded concept. In this new world, the only way to survive is to follow religiously, relentlessly, Ezra Pound's dictum, 'Make it new.'"

At least in the early days of video, the situation encouraged artistic anarchy. You "just threw a lot of stuff on the wall and saw what stuck," says Mulcahy. "There was no chart to tell you what was good and what was not. A lot of time it just came straight from the gut. It never came from an intellectual sense. It came from listening to the song. That would usually produce one single image in my head and then you would expand intellectually from that."

Because videos were produced with the goal of being seen in heavy rotation, he continues, a director must "pack as much into a clip as possible with editing

and imagery so that people can see the clip over and over and still be noticing things they never noticed before."

Because many of the videos harness these embedded and often deceptively sophisticated layers of texture and meaning into their veneer, watching videos is hardly a passive experience. Rather than destroy the viewer's ability to interpret the song, many video directors deliberately design the video to elicit an open-ended response.

"I always prefer to stay away from a literal approach to the song," Mulcahy has said. "I take it to another level, where people can take it wherever they want. You build that abstract, noncommittal quality in there to give it a more universal appeal because if people can figure it out, they get bored with it. You want to keep them intrigued."

As a result, the best videos rely far more on experimentation than on formula. Brian Grant once explained, in the early days, "There weren't any rules. Somebody was actually paying you to experiment. We were all watching each other. You saw where a technique would go and maybe you'd steal it or invent one of your own. There weren't any reference points, no library of videos so you could do what you wanted, given the budget. We were learning on the job. It was fun."

While those days of wholesale experimentation are probably over, music video remains an incredibly pliant form. Despite its reputation for being derivative, it has proven extremely adaptable. Like other contemporary mediagenic subcultures, such as skateboarding and surfing, video has become very successful at sampling images from our collective past via the intelligent use of technology.

Although talking specifically about web technology, Bowie could easily have been talking about music videos when he explained that "cutting up and taking and sampling

>> "Few other genres are as open to audience interpretation as are experiential, highly impressionistic music videos."

— LISA ST. CLAIR HARVEY, "TEMPORARY INSANITY," JOURNAL OF POPULAR CULTURE, V. 24, NO. 1, 1990

edit.

LOVECATS

THE CURE   1983

<< | TIM POPE |

| LESLIE LIBMAN & LARRY WILLIAMS | >>

MAD ABOUT YOU

BELINDA CARLISLE   1986

— even ideas — and rematching and making hybrids of what is already out there is what I have always done. . . . That is the basis of post-modernism — not attaching a backtext to history, but retrieving things from history in their most pure and pristine state."

In certain instances, this shock of the familiar gives the video its power. Spike Jonze's rendering of Weezer's "Buddy Holly," for example, makes it impossible to watch *Happy Days* through any other eyes but Jonze's again. Similarly, Julian Temple's "When I Think of You" compresses the arc of an entire M-G-M musical into one five-minute section. In the same way, "Beat It" revitalizes *West Side Story,* and Madonna's collected work is a Cliff's Notes to cinema history.

In other cases, it is the glimpse of tomorrow that is mesmerizing. Over the past fifteen years, the music video has unleased a quiver of high-tech effects that have changed the way we see the world. Even a partial list of innovations is impressive: Morphing, which most people first saw in a Godley and Crème video, "Cry"; the transformation of live-action characters to and from animated characters in Steve Barron's video of a-ha's "Take On Me"; the use of ADO (Ampex Digital Optics) in videos such as the Motels' "Only the Lonely," which allowed optical distortion and movement; and the paintbox, in which an image could be painted over live action, as in "Money for Nothing." All made their first splash in video.

This blend of old school and new, of performance and art, of abstract and literal, explains why you cannot watch just one video and why you cannot walk away thinking the videos all blur together. As Fuller wrote in *Interview,* "Music television remains as fiendishly addictive and as spiritually enervating as pornography, through its constant promise of what the next three minutes may bring. Catch yourself tuning in for a second and the next few hours whiz by like clouds in time-lapse photography."

Perhaps it is this ability to mesmerize the viewer that is partially responsible for video's bad rap. Because it goes by so quickly, you hardly know what hit you. Until now. This book purposely disrupts that flow. By freeze-framing the images, we can finally present a clear perspective on the art that has defined our visual landscape for the past twenty years. The art has been there all along. All we had to do to see it was hit "Pause."

>> "These video records are more than just a tape of a band playing and singing. They are highly stylized visual interpretations of the music, using the most advanced video techniques. And the sound is transmitted through stereo speakers, bringing a whole new dimension to the way people watch TV."
— MTV PROMOTIONAL MATERIAL, 1981

0:00:29

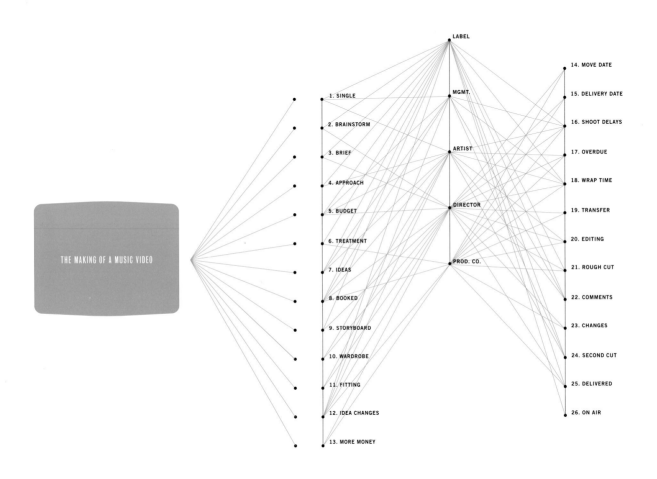

THE MAKING OF A MUSIC VIDEO

LABEL

MGMT.

ARTIST

DIRECTOR

PROD. CO.

1. SINGLE
2. BRAINSTORM
3. BRIEF
4. APPROACH
5. BUDGET
6. TREATMENT
7. IDEAS
8. BOOKED
9. STORYBOARD
10. WARDROBE
11. FITTING
12. IDEA CHANGES
13. MORE MONEY

14. MOVE DATE
15. DELIVERY DATE
16. SHOOT DELAYS
17. OVERDUE
18. WRAP TIME
19. TRANSFER
20. EDITING
21. ROUGH CUT
22. COMMENTS
23. CHANGES
24. SECOND CUT
25. DELIVERED
26. ON AIR

diagram.   above   #1-26

process.

1. Label, artist, management agree on a single. **2.** Video commissioner brainstorms on appropriate directors. **3.** Video commissioner sends a package with: music, specs/brief on creative needs, existing album art/photos to directors. **4.** Phone conversation with commissioner and artist takes place to get everyone's take on approach. **5.** Treatments are written, budgets are done. **6.** Production company submits treatment and budget to label. **7.** Label, manager, and artist determine which ideas are appropriate and...**8.** Job is booked! **9.** Storyboards and location photos are submitted to label. **10.** Wardrobe discussions between artist and director. **11.** Wardrobe fittings. **12.** Idea changes as it's discovered that locations don't come through (for money reasons, generally!), or people (on all sides) have sat with the idea for too long and now begin to inject their own "new" ideas. **13.** Director/production company determine they need more money than originally agreed to (contracted for) as "things have changed..." **14.** Shoot dates move up and back. **15.** Delivery date moves up and back. **16.** Shoot date arrives and there are delays (for a number of reasons!). **17.** Shoot day goes long due to above-mentioned delays. **18.** Wrap time actually does arrive but there's no celebrating with a "wrap beer" for fear that production or label will be found liable in event of an accident during wrap or on the drive home. **19.** Transfer of film to tape takes place in an all-night session (as that's the least expensive way to complete this transfer process). **20.** Editing begins. **21.** 2-3 days (sometimes 5-8 days) later a first rough cut is submitted by the director and production company to label. **22.** Label, artist, and manager make comments on what they want changed. **23.** Changes are made. **24.** Label, artist, and manager view second cut and determine if more changes need to be made; if so, ideally, they are minor and can be done in the on-line; video is on-lined/visual effects finished (if there are any). **25.** Video is delivered to label. **26.** Label promotions department gets it on air.

1   2   3
label.

4   5
video delivery.   shoot date.
                editing.   rough cut.

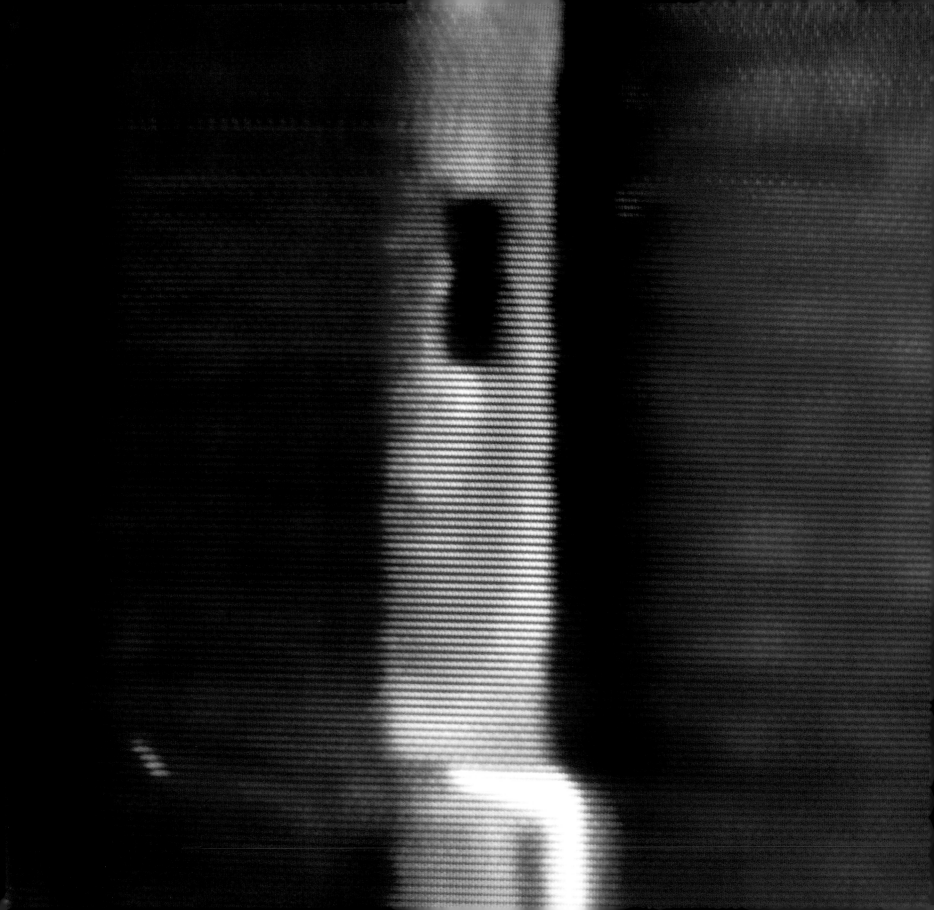

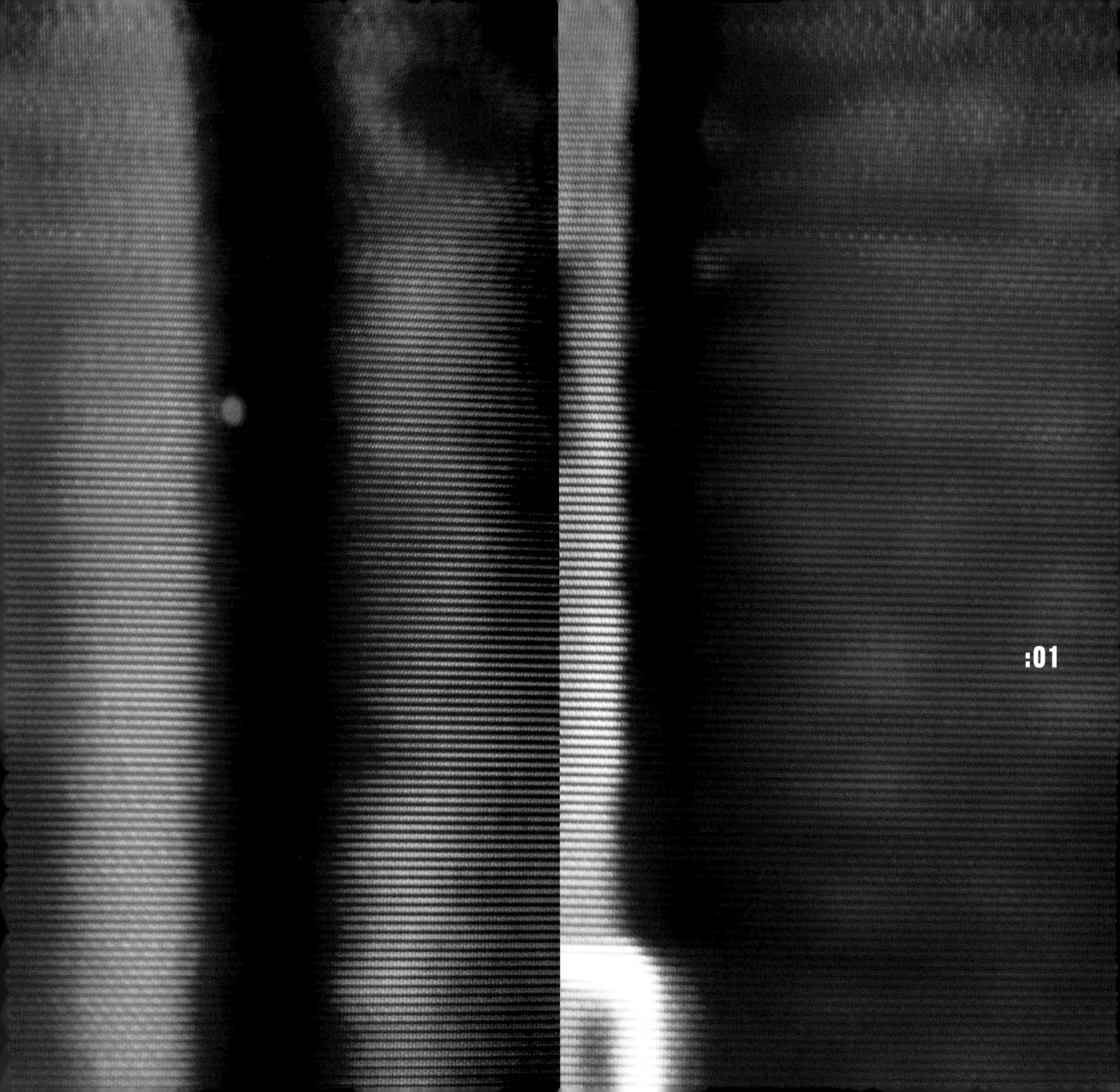
:01

RAY OF LIGHT

MADONNA

1998

<< >>

director.	**JONAS AKERLUND**			04.987	/	/	2.89		positive		3.58		video	r-90/	g-60/	b-90/	>>
		treatment.	storyboard.				hi-contrast.	sto mo.		freeze frame.	on-line.			color balance.		edit.	

bio.   Talk about range, Swedish prodigy Jonas Akerlund accomplished one of video's most divergent assaults on popular attention with the back-to-back releases of Prodigy's "Smack My Bitch Up" and Madonna's "Ray of Light."

If this yin-yang approach seemed to come from nowhere, that is only because Akerlund spent ten years cutting his teeth in the relatively remote locale of Sweden, where he was born in 1965. He had worked in the Swedish film industry since he turned twenty-one, first as a director's assistant for Anders Skog, and then as a director in his own right.

Akerlund made his first real splash with a TV documentary on Marie Fredriksson, the singer for Roxette, in 1992. He subsequently directed a handful of other videos for Roxette, Fredriksson, and other Swedish music acts, but spent most of his time directing commercials for clients such as Shell, and making a short film, *The Hidden*. Despite or because of the film's self-described "psychotic" nature, it caught the attention of Billy Poveda, the executive producer of Oil Factory Inc., which led to Akerlund's music video work with artists such as Moby, Prodigy, Metallica, and Madonna.

The Prodigy and Madonna videos remain startling bookends that define Akerlund's reach. "Smack My Bitch Up" is strong stuff and caused a storm of controversy not seen since Madonna's *Sex* days. Ironically, at the same time Prodigy were proving that they were devil's children, Madonna was in the process of transforming herself, in MTV's words, from hip-hop to "hip holy" mother. "Ray of Light" reflected that transition beautifully. Perhaps because of the positive vibrations emanating from it, that video, not Prodigy's, swept most of the video awards that year. Regardless, it is a tribute to Akerlund's vision that he was able to capture two divergent yet pitch-perfect snapshots of artists at critical junctures in their careers.

0:00:37

director. **GEOFFREY BARISH**

00.03.56   2.87

split screen.   composite.   non-linear.

bio. Like several other noted music video directors, Geoffrey Barish first established himself as a fine-art photographer. His initial exposure came as a result of his style with portraits and landscape, which, before long, caught the attention of the fashion press. But after working with clients such as Italian *Vogue, Interview, Glamour, Lei, Mademoiselle,* Ralph Lauren, and J. Crew, he decided that fashion was not where he wanted to build a career.

Instead, in 1985, he moved to Santa Fe, New Mexico, attended the Anthropology Film Center, and, while there, completed a short film, *The Cowboys of Paniola*. Keeping a home in New Mexico, he then moved to Los Angeles and started directing music videos for artists such as John Hiatt, Chris Isaak, Joan Armatrading, Don Henley, Warren Zevon, and Lenny Kravitz (with whom he also made a documentary).

His work with these artists struck a chord with Jeff Ayeroff, who was then at Virgin Records. With Ayeroff's encouragement and support, Barish produced and directed his first featurette, called *Tres Cruces*. The film played the festival circuit and helped launch his career as a TV commercial director, which spawned a number of award-winning commercials.

Barish has an atypically literary bent, which helps explain why his videography includes some of the country's most lyrical musicians, and this is why his videos so adroitly capture the magic of his locations and the emotions and stories behind the faces of "real" people. This can be traced to two big influences. The first is classic American cinema of the late 1960s and early 1970s. "When I was about ten, I saw *Bonnie and Clyde* twenty times." Films like it, *The Graduate, One Flew Over the Cuckoo's Nest,* and *Midnight Cowboy,* "were real, with good stories. No flash, and they had great characters."

His second great influence is, simply, "Life. My career isn't the most important thing. I never cared about careers. It's probably not politically right to admit that. The bottom line is, I just care about making stuff." And collaborating. "I love collaborating with everybody."

640 x 480.

steadi cam.   tracking shot.   final master.   edit.

shoot   1 2 3   4 5

HAVE A LITTLE FAITH

<< **JOHN HIATT** *1987* ∨

/ influence. /   >>

"Ain't life grand?"
— Bonnie and Clyde

MR. CAB DRIVER

<<   **LENNY KRAVITZ**

1990

director. **SAMUEL BAYER**

0.45   on-line
       dailies.

00.08.52

fast forward.   pause.

bio.   If he were to do nothing else, Samuel Bayer would have a place in history as the person who gave an entire generation's sound a look. We are talking, of course, about his video for Nirvana's anthem, "Smells Like Teen Spirit." Nominated for MTV Best Video of 1992 and winner of Best New Artist and Best Alternative Video, it remains one of the most popular videos ever made and, almost a decade later, still retains an awesome, irresistible power.

Bayer's work can be seen as a direct progression from his days in New York in the late 1980s as a struggling painter. A graduate of the School of Visual Arts, he paid the rent by illustrating album covers. His design sensibility and his high-spirited personality made him a natural candidate for music videos and enabled him to form an immediate bond with the [then] equally unknown band, Nirvana.

Working on a shoestring budget, Bayer also functioned as the video's art director and director of photography. This helps explain why he has become known for his stylized visuals and his ability to capture the "organic essence" of an artist and a song.

Not one to rest on his laurels, Bayer has since worked with a diverse group of major artists such as Blind Melon, Melissa Etheridge, Offspring, Bad Brains, David Bowie, Garbage, Smashing Pumpkins, and Metallica (on "Until It Sleeps," MTV's Best Hard Rock Video of 1996).

In addition to videos, Bayer has directed numerous commercials for clients such as Nike, Mountain Dew, Packard Bell, and Coca-Cola; and he continues to do as many non-profit public service spots as his schedule allows.

And although Bayer has long since passed from the ranks of struggling artists, he feels he has kept his goals intact. "With six years of trying, I never managed to get one of my paintings into a gallery, yet all the people I was jealous of in the art world now want to do what I'm doing. They all want to be filmmakers because the medium reaches so many more people. That's why I think I'm still an artist. If people are forced to look at your work on the millions of television sets around America, you're forcing art down their throats whether they like it or not." Smells like teen spirit, and we like it.

HOME

>> *SHERYL CROW*   1997

BULLET WITH BUTTERFLY WINGS

>> *SMASHING PUMPKINS*
1995

STUPID GIRL

rgb.

2 3 4 5

treatment.

storyboard.

off-line	4.03	10 45 8
colorist.	prep.	posterize.	one-light.

director. **BIG TV!**

/ influence. /   >>

*"This is a high-concept performance video with a unique visual twist. We will combine a '60s and '90s vision
in the same frame. For example, a wide shot of the street will show buildings, cars, shops, sign posts,
and people all styled in the '60s, whilst the right will reveal a '90s vision of the same street. . . . Only Lauryn
will exist in both worlds. She is our narrator. She crosses the divide of time."*
— From the treatment of "Doo Wop," draft three

DOO-WOP (THAT) THING
LAURYN HILL   1998

bio.   Big TV! is actually a team of two longtime friends, Andy Delaney and Monty Whitebloom. Delaney was born in Kaduna, Africa; Whitebloom, in Versailles, France. They met while at Goldsmiths College in London, where the former was majoring in multi-media studies and the latter, English literature. Both were a part of the Frieze group, which also included artist Damien Hirst.

Initially they did not think about doing promotional music videos. Instead, they took the loftier road, concentrating on video art exhibits at various London galleries and at the London and Edinburgh Film Festivals, and on video installations for London nightclubs in the late 1980s. Their nightclub connections were their entry into promotional films for fashion designers such as John Richmond, Maria Cornejo, Dries Van Noten, Dirk Birkkbergen, and Martine Sitbon, and to shooting a music video for the then obscure house band, The Beloved.

This led to the breakthrough video "Back to Life" for fashion-drenched Soul II Soul. Since then, Big TV! has worked regularly on both sides of the Atlantic with artists such as Sinead O'Connor, Lauryn Hill, Enigma, and the Spice Girls. As an account in the trade journal *Shoot* of their video for Boz Scaggs's "Some Change" shows, experience has not made a dent in their kids-in-clubland enthusiasm or resourcefulness.

They had just returned from a trip stateside, where they were to be compiling a showreel, when Scaggs called. Although the budget was far from lavish and they had barely gotten resettled, "the bags were packed before the phone went down."

The idea for the video was to make "a modern blues video. A man, a bench, a guitar, a city. We wanted to keep the man constant while we explored a city that was constantly changing around him," says Whitebloom. "We wanted this to happen imperceptibly, by creating a natural, organic effect."

Normally that would not be difficult. But financial restrictions prevented them from shooting so that the various backgrounds matched. To compensate, they had to "finesse each scene using a combination of 'averaging,' air brushing, and sky-replacement. This soothed out any bumps in the track and instilled a dreamlike quality into the city of Los Angeles." Industry credentials notwithstanding, the scrambling they did was not much different from what they did a decade earlier in the clubs. It just goes to show that you can take the boys out of the dance, but you can't take the dance out of the boys.

THREE MARLENAS

<<   THE WALLFLOWERS

1997   >>

director. **GAVIN BOWDEN**　casting.　run and gun style. 3.90　720 x 486 switcher. // // rewind.

bio.　Say what you will, family connections often come in handy. In Gavin Bowden's case, they actually led to a career. The Red Hot Chili Peppers were going to film a clip for their song "Warped" but did not have a written concept for it. Bowden knew the band, through Flea, his brother-in-law. As it sometimes does, access made for a perfect opportunity.

"I scratched a few set drawings on bits of paper that I showed to them at a restaurant," he says. "I don't think anyone really understood exactly what I was proposing, but they liked and trusted me and so agreed. If I had submitted this concept in the normal way and to a band that I didn't know, I can't imagine that anyone would have let me make it. After all, I hadn't made a 'real' video before."

The video garnered considerable attention and got him on his way. His credits include five more Chili Peppers videos, including "Coffee Shop," "Aeroplane," "My Friends," "Suck My Kiss," and "If You Have to Ask," as well as work for numerous other bands, such as Matchbox 20 ("3 A.M."), the Rollins Band ("End of Something"), Live ("Lakini's Juice"), Fun Lovin' Criminals ("Scooby Snacks"), and Rage Against the Machine ("No Shelter").

As this extract from his treatment from that Rage video demonstrates, Bowden is a director who, above all, listens to the song:

This video seeks inspiration from murals painted by Diego Rivera between 1931 and 1933 in the U.S.A. The video will achieve a disturbing image of how America's destiny is so dramatically shaped by the forces of production and consumerism, and how we have become enslaved by this system. Elements of these murals will be adapted and brought to life to create this nightmarish story of optimism, oppression, and production. These highly stylized images will be staged and filmed to capture the energy and passion of the band.

Set designs will adapt the style of Rivera's murals. . . . Wardrobe, casting, make-up etc. will follow the 1930s period but will mix this period with more modern and generic styles. Lighting is a dusty pale glow. It is like a fine veil of dust has settled on everything. These images feel oppressive and cynical yet at the same time push our imagination. There is an upsetting sense of balance between the people and their machines.

The next line in the treatment is about the video, but it could apply equally well to the form itself. In Bowden's words, "It is like we are looking into the past and the future at the same time."

RED HOT CHILI PEPPERS

WARPED

1995   >>

/ influence. /   >>

"Some scenes show cryptic images of American history with regards to oppression of Labor unions and minorities. These images are haunting. They include the bizarre portraits of Sacco and Vanzetti, the victims of labor union struggles who were electrocuted after scandalous proceedings. The faces of the nine black men falsely imprisoned for the rape of two white prostitutes are tragically displayed in a book case. A man is lashed by a whip in front of the Statue of Liberty and a line of women are chained into an unstoppable production line."
— From the treatment of "No Shelter"

bio.   Paul Boyd was born in Glasgow, Scotland, in 1967 to a working-class family. He got a Super-8 camera when he was nine and spent the next six years making experimental home movies. Without any grand plan, these videos soon evolved into home-made music videos for local bands. At seventeen, he was accepted at Middlesex Polytechnic in London, where he took a foundation course in fine art. He then matriculated into St. Martins School of Art, where he excelled, and later went to the Royal Academy of Dramatic Art, where he received a postgraduate degree.

It was at St. Martins that Boyd directed his first 16mm short film with sound, *The Thief,* and his first professional music video, for Leila K. After he finished school, he directed more than forty music videos in two years. Then, at twenty-three, he moved to Los Angeles with the express purpose of pursuing a career in feature films.

Although he has never lost sight of that goal, he continues to work steadily in music videos. He has, in fact, more than one hundred music videos to his credit, including those for artists such as Lenny Kravitz, Jamiroquai, Seal, INXS, Shania Twain, Sting, Bryan Adams, Jewel, and Tina Turner.

visual effects.   53.902

tracking shot.   rewind

rough cut.

composite.   09:43:02

director.   **PAUL BOYD**

A PRAYER FOR THE DYING
SEAL
1994   >>

bio.   Peter Care has a lower public profile than many directors of his caliber. Within the industry, however, he has been one of the most respected video artists for almost two decades. He fell into the then-emerging field from his experience as a film student at City Polytechnic in Sheffield, North England. After graduating with honors from the fine arts department, he used funding from the Arts Council and Channel 4 to write, direct, and edit several films. One, *Johnny Yesno,* used the music of Cabaret Voltaire for the soundtrack.

    The band was so impressed that they asked Care to direct some music videos for them. That led to a series of early, still-influential videos for other bands in the industrial music scene, such as Killing Joke, Peter Murphy, Thomas Dolby, Depeche Mode, Scritti Politti, and ABC.

    By 1992, Care had moved to Los Angeles, where he quickly established himself as a director who could juggle in a most painterly way. He has worked with everyone from Robbie Nevil (the one-hit wonder of "C'est La Vie") to Roy Orbison and Tom Petty to soul popster Johnny Gill to Anita Baker and Tina Turner

("What You Get Is What You See," "I Don't Wanna Fight," and "Why Must We Wait Until Tonight"). He is able to move effortlessly from genre to genre and personality to personality because he is still an art student in the best sense of the word. Rather than become jaded or enslaved by his past, he has a wide range of historical references to draw upon and is still willing to take chances.

    This risk-taking is evident in what may be Care's finest achievements, his R.E.M. "trilogy": "Drive," "Man on the Moon," and "What's the Frequency, Kenneth?" In the latter video, Care took a tremendous chance by letting the camera chase the band, and especially Michael Stipe, never really placing them full-frame. "Drive," one of the most startling concert videos ever, captures the reverential nature of the relationship of the fan to the artist in a way that no other video ever has. And "Man on the Moon," a haunting, lyrical mood piece, ultimately says more about Andy Kauffman's legacy than the movie of the same name. The comparison is a stronger testament to the power of music video than Hollywood would care to admit.

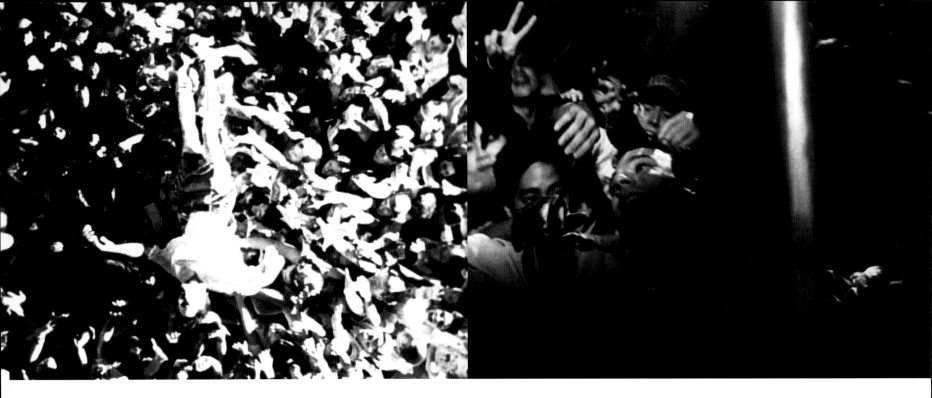

DRIVE
^ R.E.M.   1992
^

IT'S GOOD TO BE KING
TOM PETTY   >>
1995

0:00:60

/ influence: /   >>

"Peter has this ability to take a simple idea and then use his bag of tricks to come up with layers and sensibilities.
I would say something like 'let's do a walking video through the desert' and then I would add, 'oh, yeah,
throw in Andy Kaufman,' and then Peter would turn it into 'Man in the Moon.'"

– Michael Stipe

WHAT'S THE FREQUENCY, KENNETH?

>>   **R.E.M.**

1994

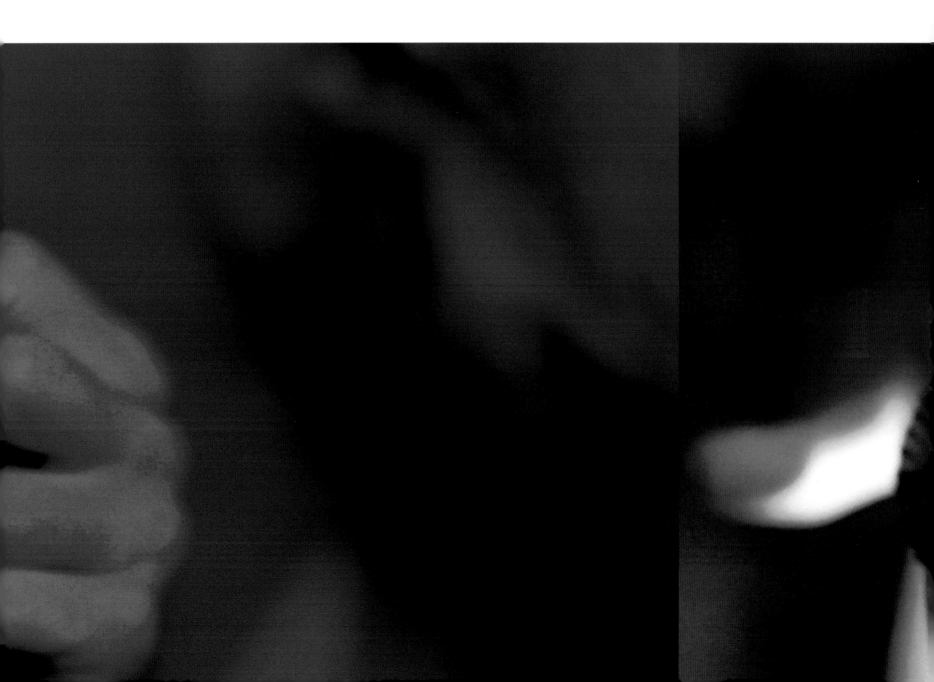

director.	ANTON CORBIJN	edit	shoot			7.20	00.08.28
		composite.	one-light.	job#.	pause.	620 x 480	dailies.	lipsync.

bio. Of the handful of still photographers who have made their mark on music videos, Dutch photographer Anton Corbijn is perhaps the only one who comes straight out of the music press — and who became a photographer because of his love of music.

His epiphany came in 1972, when the seventeen-year-old minister's son picked up his father's camera at an open-air concert. That was enough, according to his biography, to "hook him on photographing music straight away."

In the late 1970s and early 1980s, London was the center of the post-punk movement. Since his favorite music was coming from bands such as Joy Division, Magazine, and P.I.L., he moved there in 1979, just to be close to the scene.

Few venues provided access to the bands better than the magazine *NME (New Musical Express)*. Luckily, Corbijn landed a staff position, and he worked there until 1985. During that time, he befriended bands such as U2 and Depeche Mode and slowly developed a love for photography that enhanced his love of music. By the time Corbijn left *NME,* his work had already become a fixture in magazines such as *Rolling Stone, Elle, W,* and *Stern,* and he had shot covers for musicians such as U2, R.E.M., John Lee Hooker, Bryan Ferry, Nick Cave, and the Rolling Stones. He had also become identified with a trademark style, characterized by a preference for dense black-and-white images that balance a religious feel and dark romanticism with unexpected touches of humor.

By then, he had also moved into videos, beginning with the Art of Noise's "Beatbox." Although he was best known as a still photographer, a rapid succession of groundbreaking videos for Depeche Mode and Echo and the Bunnymen soon broadened his reputation as a video director as well. In the years since, he has made more than sixty videos with a roster of artists, including Nirvana (the award-winning "Heart Shaped Box"), Joni Mitchell, Henry Rollins, Metallica, Naomi Campbell, Johnny Cash, and Nick Cave.

Corbijn's success has something to do with his ability to inspire trust in his subjects. As Front 242's Jean-Luc DeMeyer says, "We don't know anything about video. We would like to but we never had time and it's very complicated and very expensive. So we decided instead of controlling even a part of it, to leave complete freedom to [Corbijn]. And we were really surprised because [the video] was absolutely not what we expected. But it was absolutely coherent with the music." End of story.

HEART SHAPED BOX

<<   NIRVANA   1993   >>

0:00:68

ROLLINS BAND   LIAR
                 1994

<<   >>

F R O Z E N

MADONNA   1998

director. **CHRIS CUNNINGHAM**

bio. Few people have come to music video with as distinguished a pedigree as Chris Cunningham. At seventeen, he was already leading the FX team on David Fincher's *Aliens 3*. Shortly thereafter, he worked with Stanley Kubrick on six robot designs for a film that was never made, and later came up with the Mean Machine character for Judge Dredd.

While he did not need the work, his passion for music ultimately drove him into music videos. "I sat down and thought, 'How can I do something that involves music?' I never particularly wanted to be a music video director or a film director, but to be involved with music. It seemed like the natural thing to do."

His first, for the techno band Autechre, was selected as best low-budget video by Music Week 1995. It was followed by a string of other startling videos, including the Aphex Twin's "Come to Daddy" (MCM grand prix du jury,

1997; Best Video, Best Cinematography, Best Editing, Music Week, 1997) and Portishead's "Only You" (nominated for Best Video, MVPA, 1997).

Those videos, not to mention Madonna's "Frozen," Björk's "All Is Full of Love," or his short-form work with artists like Placebo and Leftfield, have given him a reputation for being dark and exhibiting a cruel sense of humor. Cunningham prefers to think of his aesthetic instead as one that captures the truth behind the music. "I react strictly to the music," he says. "With some music, the emotional impact is so strong that you're busy experiencing the emotion and not seeing pictures. But other tracks put images in your head and almost have a sequential quality to them. I try to translate the emotional resonance of those songs into pictures."

"Pictures," he adds, "that are true and that are appropriate."

COME ON MY SELECTOR

<<   SQUAREPUSHER   >>

1997

/ influence. /   >>

"The problem with creating by committee is that if even just one idiot in a room full of viewers says 'OOOH that could be a little dangerous,' then everyone tends to go down the same path. That is to say that commercial art tends to cater to the lowest common denominator. The few music videos that are truly inspirational, like Chris [Cunningham's] Björk, Jake [Scott's] U2, or Mark [Romanek's] NIN, were created in an environment where the director and the artist overrided everyone else's opinion. That's the only way to remain pure, therefore remembered."
– Rhea Rupert, Executive Producer, Little Minx

APHEX TWIN

COME TO DADDY

1997

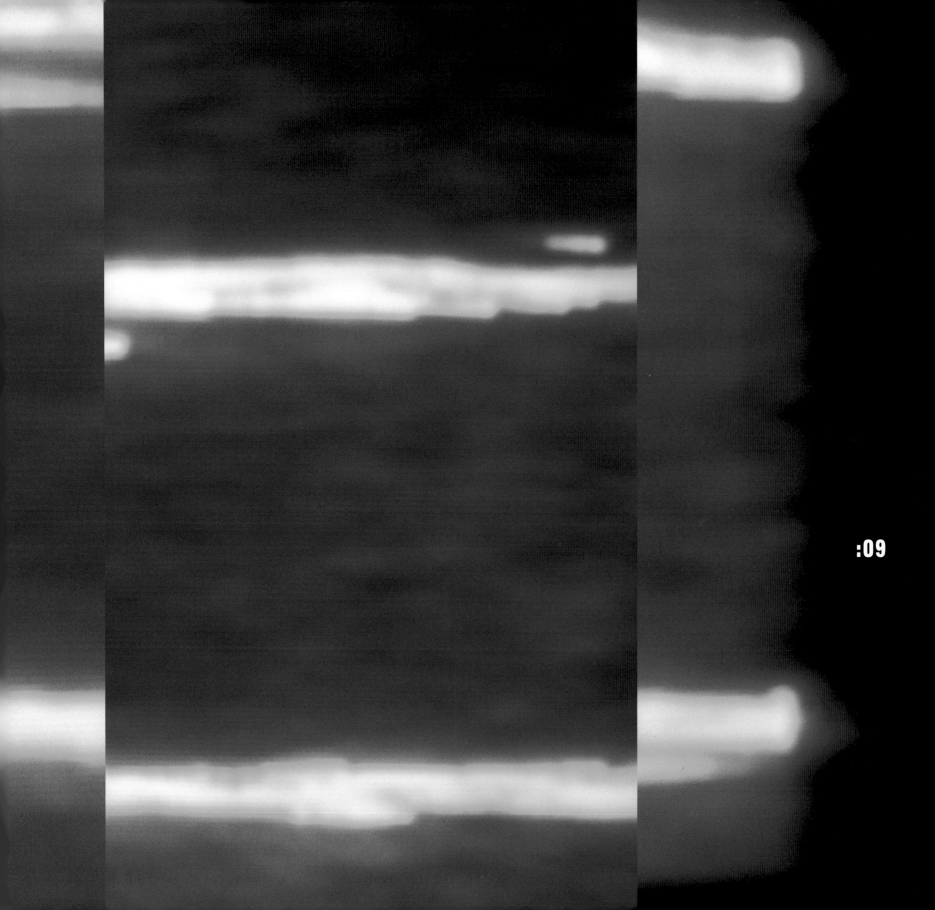

bio. As Tamra Davis can tell you, an apprenticeship with Francis Ford Coppola is not a bad beginning for a filmmaker. After working with him at Zoetrope Studio in 1986 and three years of film school at Los Angeles City College, Davis began directing music videos with a ferocity that landed her one of the most eclectic client lists in history: Sonic Youth, Hüsker Dü, Lou Reed, the Smiths, Depeche Mode, the Indigo Girls, New Kids on the Block, Beavis and Butthead and Cher, Hanson, Luscious Jackson, Dre, the Beastie Boys. Range, anyone?

She also helped set the pattern for numerous other video directors when she made her feature film debut with the independently produced *Guncrazy* in 1992. Featuring Drew Barrymore, it premiered at the Cannes Film Festival and toured the festival circuit before its theatrical release. On the strength of its success, Davis got her first studio feature, *CB4,* which Chris Rock wrote and starred in, and which opened as the no. 1 box-office film in America. She followed it with the Adam Sandler comedy *Billy Madison; Best Men,* again starring Drew Barrymore; and several other films, including the independent release *Skipped Parts.*

These movies are only part of the picture. In between the studio projects, Davis has directed documentaries, such as *Vida Loca,* which focuses on gang relations in the San Fernando Valley; *No Alternative Girls,* a short film starring Kim Gordon, Courtney Love, and Luscious Jackson; and *Landmines in Africa,* which was filmed for the United Nations and President Clinton's Demining 2010 Initiative.

director. **TAMRA DAVIS**

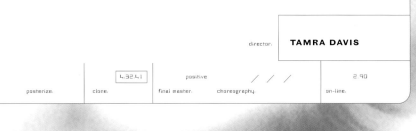

posterize. clone. `4.32.41` final master. positive choreography. / / / on-line. 2.90

VERUCA SALT ALL HAIL ME 1995

LUSCIOUS JACKSON CITYSONG 1994

LUSCIOUS JACKSON CITYSONG 1994

LUSCIOUS JACKSON CITYSONG 1994

SONIC YOUTH 100% 1992

LADYFINGERS 1999

LUSCIOUS JACKSON 1994

rewind.

off-line.

sla ma.

production design.

0:00:79

<<

SMASHING PUMPKINS

TONIGHT, TONIGHT

1996

bio.   Jonathan Dayton and Valerie Faris burst onto the scene in 1983 with MTV's breakthrough documentary program, "The Cutting Edge." A reaction against the lip-synching and artificiality of many of the early videos, it featured acoustic versions of songs, along with backstage access and live concert broadcasts.

The show was aimed at the then prevalent fear that music video would destroy rock, and it ran for five years. Its success forced Dayton and Faris to reevaluate their longstanding vow as documentary directors to never direct music videos. They cut their teeth with Janet Jackson's *Rhythm Nation: The 1814 Documentary,* which won the Long-Form Video Grammy. They have not stopped working since.

Their videos are consistently innovative, increasingly abstract, and particularly intelligent in terms of their references. Their award-winning 1996 video of the Smashing Pumpkins' epic "Tonight, Tonight" demonstrates the process by which they try to "illuminate, rather than merely illustrate the song." Initially, the two had planned on making the video a homage to Busby Berkeley and were actually in the process of hiring synchronized swimmers when they found out that the Chili Peppers had just filmed a video with a similar concept.

Regrouping, Dayton and Faris decided to reference the films of George Melies (whose name prominently appears on the ship in the video). To capture the spirit of the special-effects wizard, they used a combination of an antique hand-cranked camera and modern technology. "We were trying to revive an interest in these old films, whose air of innovation and experimentation is just as effective and magical today as it was back then," says Faris.

"We wrote the scenario with that sense of unfolding adventure and spectacle," continues Dayton. "We deliberately strayed from typical music video cutting. Instead, we wanted you to enter the scene and then study it."

While in a different visual vein, another award winner, the 1993 Porno for Pyros' "Pets," also displays their ability for conceptual and meta-phorical expression. "It was a hypnotic song, with a lot of repetition and distortion," says Dayton. Reflecting the directors' interest in cubism, the two came up with "a filmic equivalent of a cubist painting," accentuated by the use of heightened angles, female body builders, and a drill team.

Because Dayton and Faris have been pushing boundaries for almost twenty years, the pressure to live up to their reputation and to keep finding new ground to break can become a burden in and of itself. But the pressure is, Dayton says, "self-inflicted. We see people who get known for doing one thing over and over again and sometimes we wonder what it would be like."

"It probably would be easier to specialize," Faris agrees. "But it just doesn't happen that way for us."

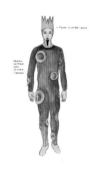

director.   **JONATHAN DAYTON & VALERIE FARIS**

<< 1979 >>
SMASHING PUMPKINS
1996

PETS
PORNO FOR PYROS *1993* >>

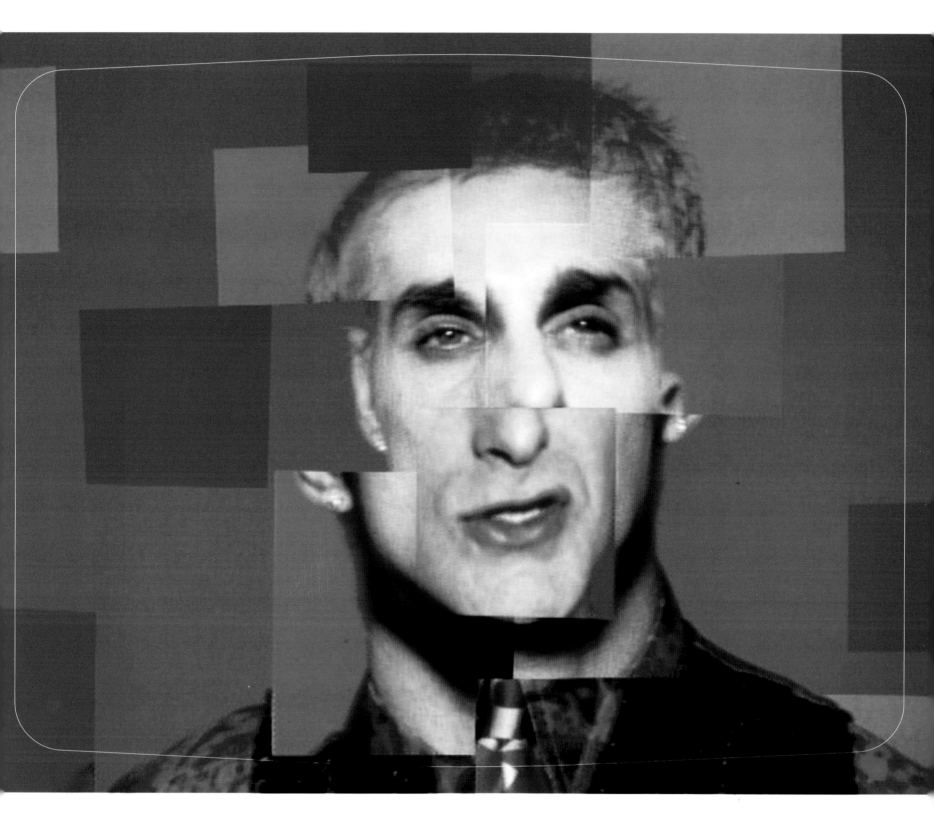

0:00:83

^

OASIS

ALL AROUND THE WORLD

1997

SHE WILL HAVE HER WAY

V
V **NEIL FINN**

1998

director. **GERARD DE THAME**   WONDERFUL LIFE
                                    ∧   **BLACK**
                                    ∧
                                                        1987

00.09.52	rgb	lipsync	/ /	0.06	video	fake type	
one-light.	720 x 486.	clone.	storyboard.	treatment.	on-line.	off-line.	visual effects.

0:00:86

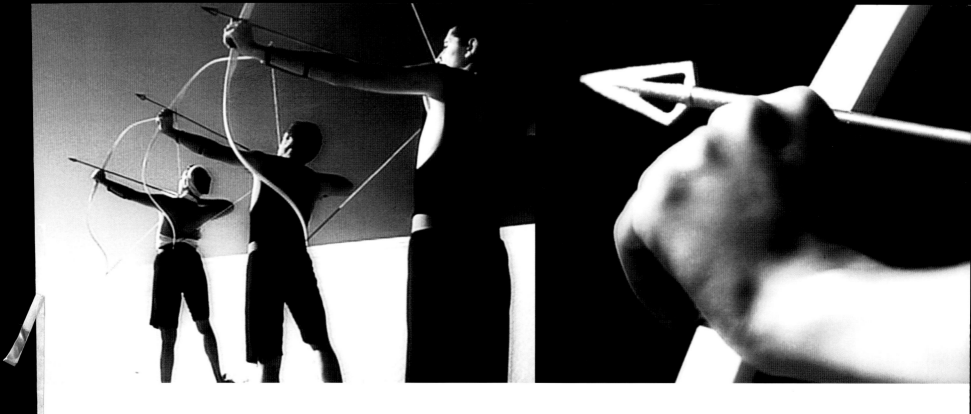

∧ **TANITA TIKARAM**

CATHEDRAL SONG

1988

bio.   Gerard de Thame's 1988 video "Wonderful Life" for the group Black typifies his style, which is best described as beautiful portraits in motion. It won a silver award in the New York Film Festival, a Diamond Award for Best Male Video, and a Golden Lion Award at Cannes in 1988. More importantly, as with his equally celebrated video the next year for Tanita Tikaram, "Twist in My Sobriety," it remains a video that video directors continually reference.

For de Thame, who graduated from London's Chelsea School of Art in the early 1980s, music video was a logical place to develop his talent. He did not stay long, however, making a jump to the ranks of blue-chip clients such as Barclay's Bank, British Telecom, Volkswagen, American Express, Mercedes-Benz, and Adidas. He has been a familiar face at awards ceremonies on both sides of the Atlantic, and has Clios and Andys flanking the Cannes Lions.

0:00:87

director. **NIGEL DICK**

3.58

mHz.   output.   input.

bio.   Veteran director Nigel Dick weighs in with more than two hundred twenty music videos, which most people believe makes him second only to Russell Mulcahy in terms of video output. His versatility as a video director, with a client list that ranges from Ozzy Osborne, Guns 'n' Roses, Oasis, and the Offspring to Celine Dion, the Backstreet Boys, and Paul McCartney, is matched only by his own eclectic background, which includes semi-professional cycling, playing the guitar, and writing (seven screenplays and a successful annual film guide).

Although also a trained architect, Dick entered music video, literally, as a motorcycle messenger for Stiff Records in London. In a new twist on the boy-in-the-mailroom story, he quickly rode the anti-corporate ladder all the way up to in-house producer. Then, true to form for Stiff, in 1985 he was fired. Somewhat bruised by the rejection, Dick decided to move to Los Angeles, where he sold a story that became the feature film *Private Investigations* and co-founded Propaganda Films.

From the beginning, he has always believed that the best videos are a combination of story and what he calls "cool stuff." In theory, at least, he likes narrative videos "because you get to make a little film." But, he continues, "all too often, when everyone sees it, they want to pull the story out and just put more close-ups of the artist in. And who's to say that they're wrong. That is what we're selling."

He has learned to anticipate this problem by blending the story with the trappings of what he calls the "cool-stuff video" format. These videos are crammed full of accessories, clothes, and visual asides, so that their style disguises the lack of substance.

"Cool-stuff videos are great because all you have to worry about is getting loads of cool stuff and start cutting so that everything goes with everything else. I feel that is a bit of a cop-out, so I try to do both at once. That way, there's some form of linear idea going on, but there's enough cool stuff to protect me when everybody gets their changes in the edit."

Like most other seasoned directors, Dick is hard-pressed to single out a favorite video, but his experience with Band Aid's "Do You Know It's Christmas" inevitably remains a high point. "It was my own personal Woodstock," he says. "I stood just feet away from Phil Collins playing the drums and heard Sting, Boy George, Paul Young, and George Michael all singing next to me without any studio trickery. Oh, yeah, we also helped save millions of lives. How often do you get to do that by making a video?"

DON'T GO AWAY

^ **OASIS**

1997

HOW'S IT GOING TO BE

I WANT YOU

THIRD EYE BLIND

SAVAGE GARDEN

1997

1997   >>

/ influence. /   >>

"In the beginning, music video was the marriage of art and commerce; it is only of late that the art was divorced."
– Joseph Uliano, Executive Producer, Crash Films

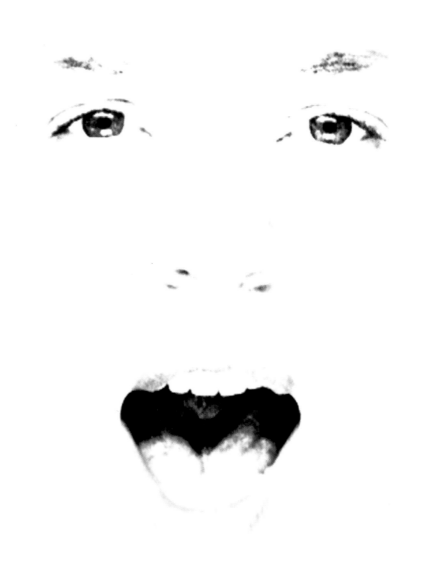

director.
Dom & Nic

		7.41.63	rewind	1.29.39
non-linear.	playback.	hi-contrast.	composite.	

rgb

clone

^ *David Bowie & Trent Reznor* **I'M AFRAID OF AMERICANS**

rough cut

1997 >>

job #

stylist dailies.

They are still young and relatively new at the game, but Nicolas Goffey and Dominic Hawley, self-described twentysomething English "upstarts," show every sign of becoming one of video's enduring directing teams. Friends since they were students at a school in Oxfordshire, England, they both fooled around on the fringes of the film business after university. Their big break came when Nic's brother's band, Supergrass, got signed to Parlophone.

Rather than shoot with a director they did not know, the band asked the two to direct the video for "Mansize Rooster." Since then, Dom & Nic have directed every Supergrass video, not to mention a handful for artists such as the Chemical Brothers, Oasis, David Bowie and Trent Reznor, and Smashing Pumpkins.

Over time, the partnership has developed organically. "We kind of split everything 50-50," says Dom. "We get together quite a bit before a shoot and do a lot of brainstorming . . . we haven't got an arrangement where one of us works with the camera and the other with the people in front of the camera. We split everything, and whoever has the best take on something, we do it that way."

The process is a logical extension of their interest in "stories and natural progressions," and of their longstanding fascination with films.

"Whenever we are directing something, we tend to go for realism. We want things to look kind of real, rather than stylized."

Sometimes, such as in the Chemical Brothers' "Setting Sun," the reality stems from putting the audience into the video. It's like being asked to step inside the hallucinatory mind of a semi-conscious raver, which quickly forces the viewer into sensory overload that feels, rather than looks, real.

Other times, the videos look and feel more like traditional cinema. According to David Bowie, who raved to the *Los Angeles Times* about his and Reznor's experience with the two on the video for the remix, "I'm Afraid of Americans," "They're a new school. A lot of video directors see everything they do as potentially a show reel for Hollywood producers. These kids really love making videos, and they are very good at getting that very British, shot-on-a-shoestring quality. They work exactly like filmmakers, doing only one or two takes, so everything looks real-time."

Dom & Nic remain loyal to and enthusiastic about music video. Bowie's take notwithstanding, they also make no secret of their ambition to impress those Hollywood producers. "We want to do a really good video more than anything," they say. "But our ambition is to direct a feature together before we die."

director.	JESSE DYLAN		620 x 480	2/9/97	dolly move			8.41	video		143 5 340 26
		final master.	casting.	non-linear.	freeze frame.		shoot.	lipsync.	edit.	storyboards.

bio: Jesse Dylan has distinguished himself as a video director, working with artists such as Tom Waits, Maria McKee, the Replacements, Tom Petty, P.I.L., Lenny Kravitz, Henry Rollins, and Nick Cave. More than most, however, he has used his music videos as a point of departure not just for commercials, but for socially relevant media.

In 1992, for instance, he worked as the creative director for the Rock the Vote campaign. In that capacity, he wrote and directed spots that included "200 Years" and "World of Tomorrow" with John Turturro. Both of these won Effie Awards in 1993. Not content to keep this forum strictly to himself, he also enlisted directors such as David Fincher and Alek Keshishian to add their own contributions to the campaign.

Continuing that vein of social responsibility, Dylan directed the "Spoken Word" exhibit for the 1993 Lollapolooza festival. For that, he included directors such as Mark Pellington and Tony Kaye; directed the Jim Carroll section; featured artists such as Pearl Jam, Nirvana, Sonic Youth, and Allen Ginsberg; and incorporated footage of Gregory Corso and Jack Kerouac.

GOIN' OUT WEST
TOM WAITS   1992

RED RIGHT HAND
NICK CAVE AND THE BAD SEEDS   1994

<<   >>

YOU OUGHTA KNOW

ALANIS MORISSETTE   1995

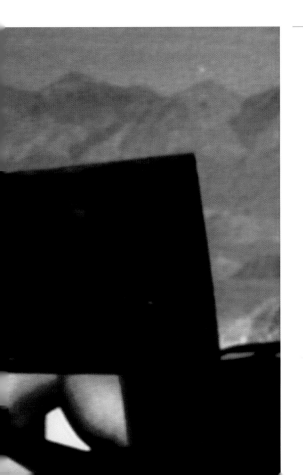

director:	**NICK EGAN**		on-line		/ / /	5/9/93
		slo mo.		dolly move.		colorist.

bio.　Nick Egan is one of those rare directors whose work spans virtually the entire history of MTV and carries with it equal success in both the print media and the social milieu that help define all aspects of the music world. His style is a self-described "spicy cauldron of music videos, British punk, and stylized graphic design for album covers, books, and fashion wear." As befitting such a grand reach, he has worked with fashion statements such as Mick Jagger and Duran Duran; punk stalwarts such as the Clash, the Sex Pistols, and Sonic Youth; and contemporary stars such as Oasis and Silverchair.

Although he is probably more closely identified with his work in commercials, Egan, like many others, got his foot in that door because of a music video. Egan's crossover break, in fact, came after advertising giant Leo Burnett saw Egan's video for the Soup Dragons's "Divine Thing," which won its year's Best Alternative Video category at the MTV Music

Video Awards. That led to a Nintendo campaign, "Play It Loud," which juxtaposed candid shots of teenagers with repressed adults; and to a Diet Coke campaign that made effective use of the then-novel technique of morphing.

A graduate of London's Warford School of Art, Egan has done considerable morphing himself. His album cover "Kick" for INXS has won numerous print awards; and he has designed books for Bob Dylan and John Lennon, album covers for Iggy Pop and the Psychedelic Furs, and logos and covers for the Clash, the Ramones, and the Sex Pistols. And although he has since worked for unpunkish clients such as Perry Ellis, Sony Playstation, Nike, and the Oak Tree (for which he developed their cool-blue and sepia look), he has retained the credibility necessary to work with today's definitive musical artists, such as Alanis Morissette ("You Oughta Know"). In this industry, a career of that length and range is indeed a divine thing.

a. b. c. d.		2.29.18				894.71	
switcher.	composite.	color balance.		steadi cam.	edit.		rough cut.

^ MANBREAK

READY OR NOT
1997

/ influence. /   >>

*"A good video DOES NOT turn your mind to mush, obliterate the imagination, or overpower the music.
It adds another dimension to the ideas being communicated. Of course, acts with no ideas in their
music tend to have none in their videos either. The trick now is to reclaim the creativity behind sight
and sound media, to insist that music and music video can and should be wonderful."
– Clark Humphrey, Wire, January 9, 1990*

BLOODCLOT
∧ RANCID

1998

director. David Fincher

☐ r
☐ ii
☐ ii

720 x 486   one-light

fast forward.   playback.

CRADLE OF LOVE
Billy Idol   1990

bio.   What can you say about David Fincher? A co-founder of Propaganda Films and one of the most respected video directors, he was one of the first to develop name recognition not just within the industry, but also among the general public. He was also the person who proved you could go from music videos to serious films, with his features *Seven* and *The Fight Club.*

Although Fincher has never made a secret of his ambition to jump to features, he has the deepest respect for music videos — at least if they are directed by someone else. "I always loved music video, but don't like most of mine," he says. "I like videos like [Madonna's] 'Oh, Father' and [the Stones'] 'Love Is Strong,' but I did most of them as my way of going to film school."

These days, he continues, filmmakers have the option of doing low-budget short films and "hawking their scripts" in ways that were not available twenty years ago. "It wasn't like I said, 'duh, I want to be the other video guy.' But at the time, in 1980, I had graduated from high school and saw videos by Russell Mulcahy and said, 'this is a great way to learn.' And it was a great sandbox."

One thing he learned from directing his videos, such as Madonna's "Vogue" and "Express Yourself," Paula Abdul's "Cold Hearted," Don Henley's "The End of Innocence," Aerosmith's "Janie's Got a Gun," and the Wallflowers' "Sixth Avenue Heartache," is that video is truly abstract. As a result, he believes videos are the most purely cinematic form. "You have carte blanche in terms of what it can show."

As a video director, he says, "Your job is to supply other interpretations, to be less specific in your references, and to provide a leap into another perspective. A video can't be so concrete that there is just one interpretation; someone is going to see it at least ten times so you better be able to give them something that they can constantly see new things in."

If for this reason alone, music video has helped improve the look of feature films. "Before 1980," says Fincher, "there were only a handful of well staged, well crafted movies a year. Because of music videos, there are more cinematographers, production designers, and more thoughtful craft people now. Movies have never looked better."

Oddly, he continues, features have been slower to make the most of the storytelling opportunities the videos allow. "Videos have helped create an audience that is willing to go with an abstract approach and is better versed and more appreciative of things that people haven't seen."

Although most movies have not picked up on that opportunity, Fincher feels films such as *Magnolia* and *Being John Malkovich* suggest an impending renaissance in storytelling, and music-video people such as Spike Jonze may be the ones to push that forward.

While Fincher continues to want to direct music videos, he admits that working in feature films makes the idea of music videos more difficult. "It's a question of shifting gears," he explains. "Movies take longer to do. Videos remind me of what the early days of the [Orson Welles] Mercury Theatre must have been like, with you burning candles at both ends and staying up for two or three nights and getting it done. With movies, you have to make compromises with your enthusiasm and energy. It's a totally different discipline, and you have to train differently. Sprinters have big thighs and long-distance runners are skinny for a reason."

treatment   on / off /
switcher.

storyboard.   1.01.59

3.79
composite.   crane shot.

0:01:02

LOVE IS STRONG

The Rolling Stones
1994

⌃

0:01:03

EXPRESS YOURSELF

^ ^ *Madonna* 1989

v
v

Madonna   **VOGUE**   1990

0:01:05

HOME
Iggy Pop   1990

FREEDOM 90
George Michael   1990   >>

v
v

/ influence: /   >>   *"Look around you and you will see that virtually every piece of visual pop culture today, from Hollywood to Madison Avenue, has in some way been affected by the talent explosion born from the art of the music video. The sheer combustion of music and film created a medium that became a talent magnet for a generation of directors and filmmakers who until that moment were without a visual voice."*
— Beth Broday, former President of both Fusion Films and N. Lee Lacy Music Video, current President of TIDAL4

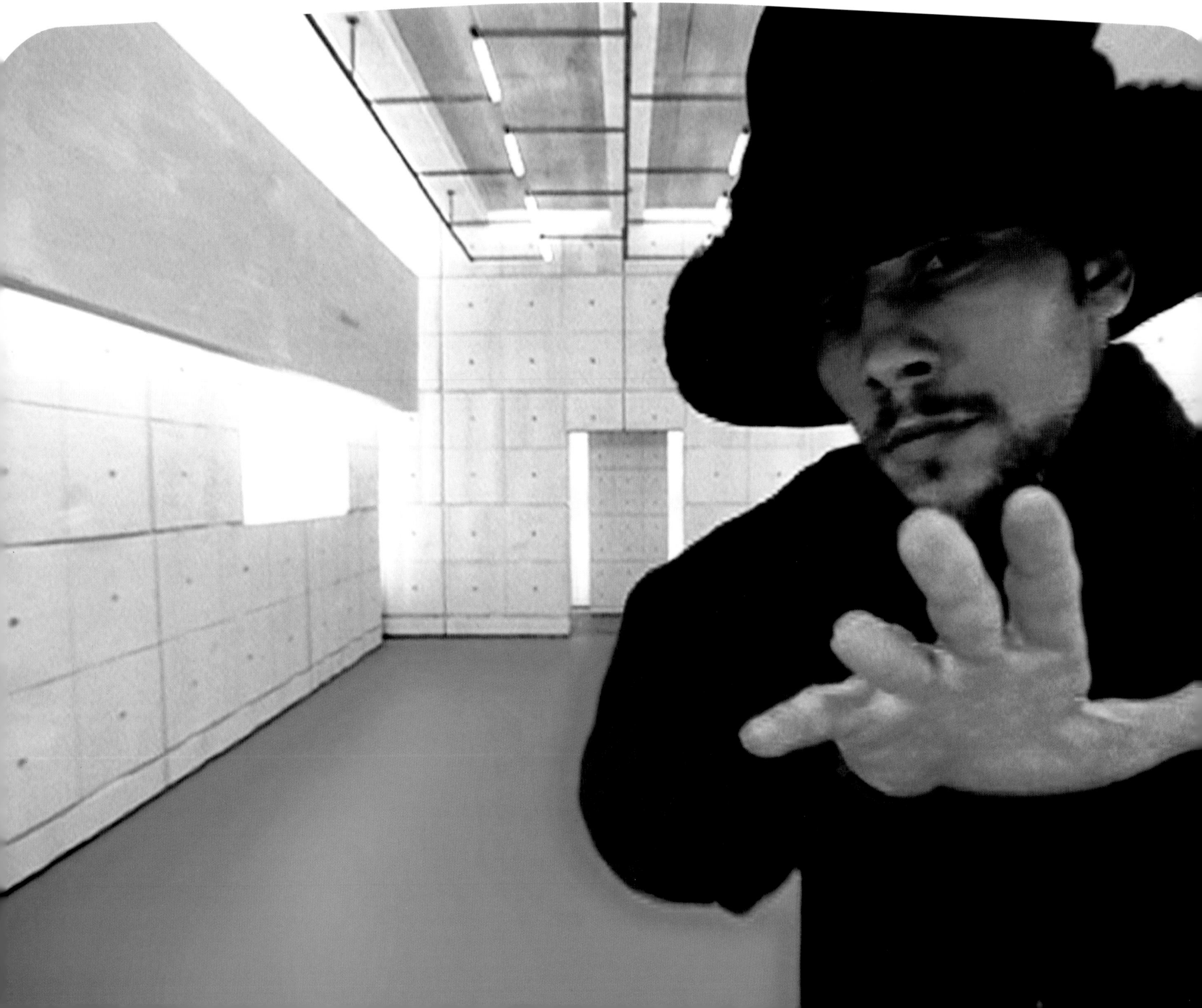

3.58   clone   1 2 4 - 720 x 1.66 lines per resolution

prep.   switcher.   luminance.   chroma.   edit.

director.   **JONATHAN GLAZER**   job#   off-line

shoot.

bio.   The stage has spawned very few video directors, but then there is very little that is typical about Jonathan Glazer. That includes his take on the music-video genre, which he once called both "rubbish" and fantastic — in the same interview.

Glazer received a bachelor-of-arts degree with honors in theater design and direction in England in the 1980s and began his career as a freelance director working in the theater. Professional opportunity was easier to find in film, however, so he soon became part of a company that made film and video trailers. Within several years, he was a senior director/writer at a different firm, creating and directing TV promos. By 1993, on the strength of two short films, "Mad" and "Pool," which he wrote and directed, he made the move into videos and commercials.

He prides himself on being selective: "I had a lot more confidence and self-belief, I think, than most new directors. And everything I've done has been very conceptual. It is a total artistic collision. Blur aside, I've shared the same sensibility as the artists I've made videos for. They do in music what I achieve in pictures."

It has been that way from the first, with Massive Attack's "Karmacoma" and, even more impressively, Radiohead's "Street Spirit," which won the Best Pop Video and a special director's award at Music Week 1996. Most impressively, Jamiroquai's "Virtual Insanity," which won Best Overall Video at the MVPA and Billboard Music Awards, got an unprecedented ten nominations for the 1997 MTV Awards, where it won Best Video, Best Cinematography, Best Special Effects, and Best Breakthrough Video.

The video was a perfect example of Glazer's confrontational approach. "Jay (Kay, the singer) said he wanted to move around on a airport baggage travelator. I thought, 'crap,' but he obviously wants to move around a lot, and that's him, isn't it?"

Kay was thrilled with the results until Glazer decided to have blood seep from under the sofa. Kay objected, feeling that the blood was out of sync with the song's mood, but Glazer was unrelenting. Kay told Glazer that he was "only there to make a video." So Glazer "kept him going for so long he was too tired to argue."

When the video aired, its special effects had the video community puzzled. Finally *Promo* magazine busted Glazer and his crew with the secret: a surprisingly simple combination of a locked-off camera bolted onto a crane, rollers under the floor, and rods under the furniture. Most people thought the effects were far more elaborate. "If you're simple, you're effective," said Glazer.

Now, about that interview. On the eve of the 1997 MTV Music Video Awards, Glazer told *Time* that music videos are "largely rubbish." But, lest anyone think he is "contemptuous" of the form, as the article accused him of being, he refused to dismiss the videos as a mere stepping stone to feature films. "I don't believe you graduate from one to another. Meeting rock stars, attending award shows — who would want to leave a film school like this?"

STREET SPIRIT
RADIOHEAD
1996

0:01:10

RADIOHEAD

KARMA POLICE

1997

V
V

director. **KEVIN GODLEY & LOL CREME**

☐ hi-contrast   ☐ crane shot

bio.   Although Kevin Godley and Lol Creme each went solo in 1989, their groundbreaking work with videos such as "Cry" (for their own song), Herbie Hancock's "Rock-It," and the Police's "Every Breath You Take" is so important in the history of music video that it is still difficult to treat the directors separately, rather than as a team.

Before they were video directors or, for that matter, technological gurus, they were musicians, first as part of the popular group 10cc and then as a duo. Their concerts were always visually oriented and their fear of technology minimal, so there is a certain retro logic to the speed with which they embraced the medium of the music video.

Godley and Creme are known as formalists with a craving for abstract patterns and wizards in post-production. In a field where the past often shows its age, certain techniques and moments still retain their power years later: the dissolves that blended photographs of faces in "Cry" (anticipating morphing by years), the multi-screened motif and the bringing to life of static images in Asia's "Heat of the Moment," and the tracking through the bazaar of candles in the Police's "Wrapped Around Your Finger."

Godley continues to direct music videos for superstar clients such as U2, Sting, and Paul McCartney; and also directs long-form projects such as the television projects *U2's Zoo TV Tour* and the two-hour *One World, One Voice.* More recently, his video for Eric Clapton's "My Father's Eyes" was nominated by the MVPA, and that for U2's "The Sweetest Thing" won the Adult Contemporary Video of the Year in 1999.

Creme, who unsuccessfully asked Walt Disney for a job when he was seven, has gone on to produce and direct award-winning high-tech commercials for clients such as Chrysler, Chevron, and Pacific Bell; and has created, coproduced, and directed a comedy series called *Limboland* for Comedy Central. In addition to keeping his hand in developing technology, such as putting Winnie the Pooh into 3-D, and becoming a digital artist, he is working with record producer Trevor Horn on a new Art of Noise album and series of videos. Even after all these years, you just can't stop the music.

ROCK-IT
GODLEY & CREME: HERBIE HANCOCK
1983

KEVIN GODLEY: FOREST FOR THE TREES   *DREAM*
                                              1997

THE SWEETEST THING

1998

U2

>>

1999

THE CHARLATANS   FOREVER

>>

<<

HUMAN BEHAVIOR   >>

BJÖRK   1993

bio.   For Michel Gondry, necessity was the mother of invention. In the early 1990s, he was a graphic art student and drummer for the French band, Oui Oui. The band had no money and no video. With no better alternative, he shot the video. It did not do much for the band's career, but it quickly became Gondry's calling card, landing him a producer and the attention of no less than Björk.

Oui Oui was formed as a reaction against the doom-and-gloom Goth bands populating art schools. Like the band, Gondry's video reflected a positive attitude but not at the expense of its underlying aggressive stance. Björk saw enough of herself in that approach to trust him with the song "Human Behavior."

She is, he learned, "one of the few people in pop music to create her own universe." Not only did she come up with the now famous bear, she also gave Gondry the freedom to create what the *New York Times* later called the best pop video ever made, "surreal without pretension, like a child's dreams and festooned with bright sets and oversized props." It was, the article concluded, an example of how "pop videos can reach the level of art while still allowing the performer her star power."

This lavish praise was heaped on a video that looked expensive but actually had a much lower budget than people thought. A testament to the fact that inspiration is more important than money, the video features a stunning hand-built forest, combines animation with rear-screen projection, and constructs a dreamlike narrative that would ultimately become a Gondry signature.

In what was also to become typical Gondry, he sandwiched a two-day shoot between lengthy periods of animation and studio work prior to the shoot and equally extensive periods of post-production. "We work in the old tradition of the artisan — the quality of work is the most important," he says. "While money is not something to sneeze at, it is not a substitute for time."

As Gondry has demonstrated ever since, "Human Behavior" was not just beginners' luck. The inventiveness of his subsequent work in videos and commercials has led to his being compared to George Melies. Like Melies, one of the most inventive of the early cinema pioneers, Gondry's special effects have been dazzling. In Terence Trent D'Arby's "She Kissed Me," for example, he brought movie stills to life. His futuristic city with people on wheels for Donald Fagen's "Snowbound" has been compared to Fritz Lang's *Metropolis;* and his video "Like a Rolling Stone" for the Rolling Stones was the first to master the technique of time suspension or so-called frozen moment (in which there is a feeling of movement around a three-dimensional subject frozen in time).

It would be a mistake, however, to peg Gondry as merely a special-effects wizard. His videos are truly collaborative, and he spends an unusual amount of time with the artists beforehand. Like Spike Jonze, who is producing Gondry's feature film, *Human Nature,* Gondry always harnesses the special effects to carefully fleshed-out structures. As Gondry says, "I always try to do something new and amusing, but it's really to serve the point of the story."

00.3.28 | 0.11 | | pause

visual effects. | prep. | rewind.

director.   **MICHEL GONDRY**

job# 0-35-1   on-line

telecine transfer. | hi-contrast.   run and gun style.

0:01:18

"Music videos have this unique ability to combine dream and reality. No boundaries, no limits, if you can imagine it, you can do it. It's freedom at its best. Musicians and filmmakers team up to write a visual book on our society. In 2099, students will look at music videos in both history and art classes. Visual effects help dreams come true. The never ending progress of what's doable fuels and helps the imagination and helps filmmakers to keep creating new visuals that blow our minds. A lot of movies and commercials started to dig into the music video world to reinvent themselves; it's a recognition of music videos as an art form."

– Alex Frisch, visual effects artist at Method, who has worked with directors Dom & Nic, Michel Gondry, Francis Lawrence, Kier McFarlane, Jean-Baptiste Mondino, Mark Romanek, and Stephane Sednaoui

SUGAR WATER
CIBO MATTO
1996

0:01:20

FOO FIGHTERS *EVERLONG* 1997

0:01:21

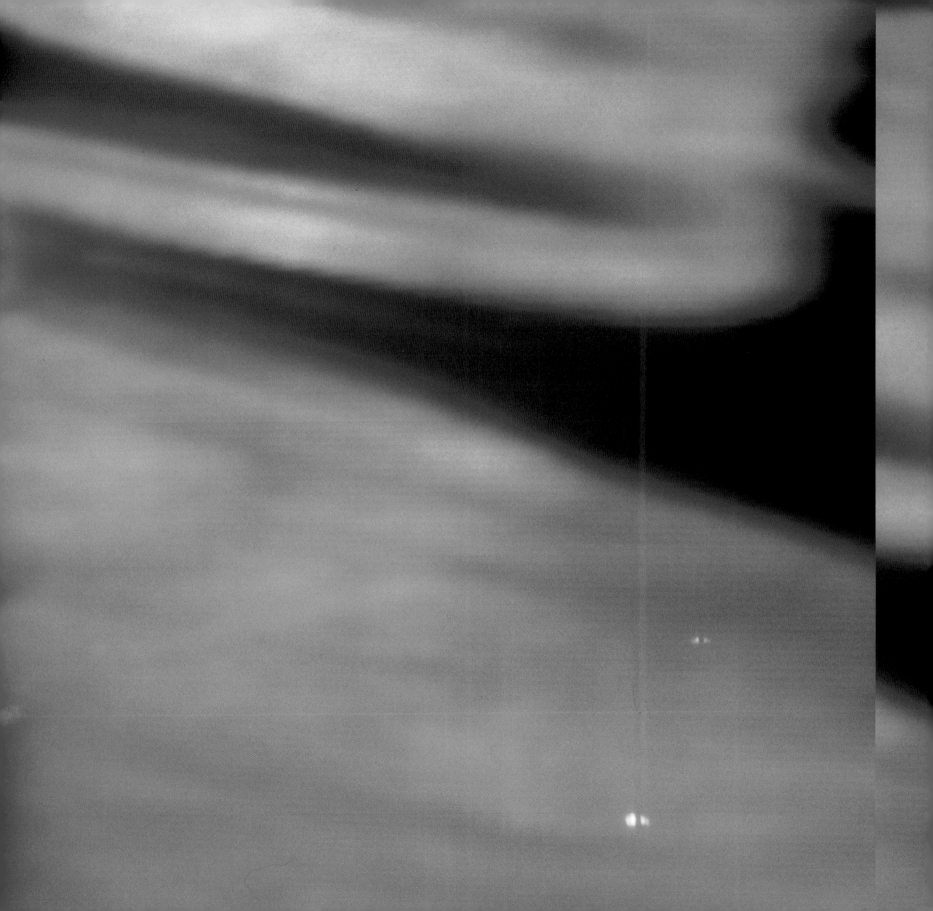

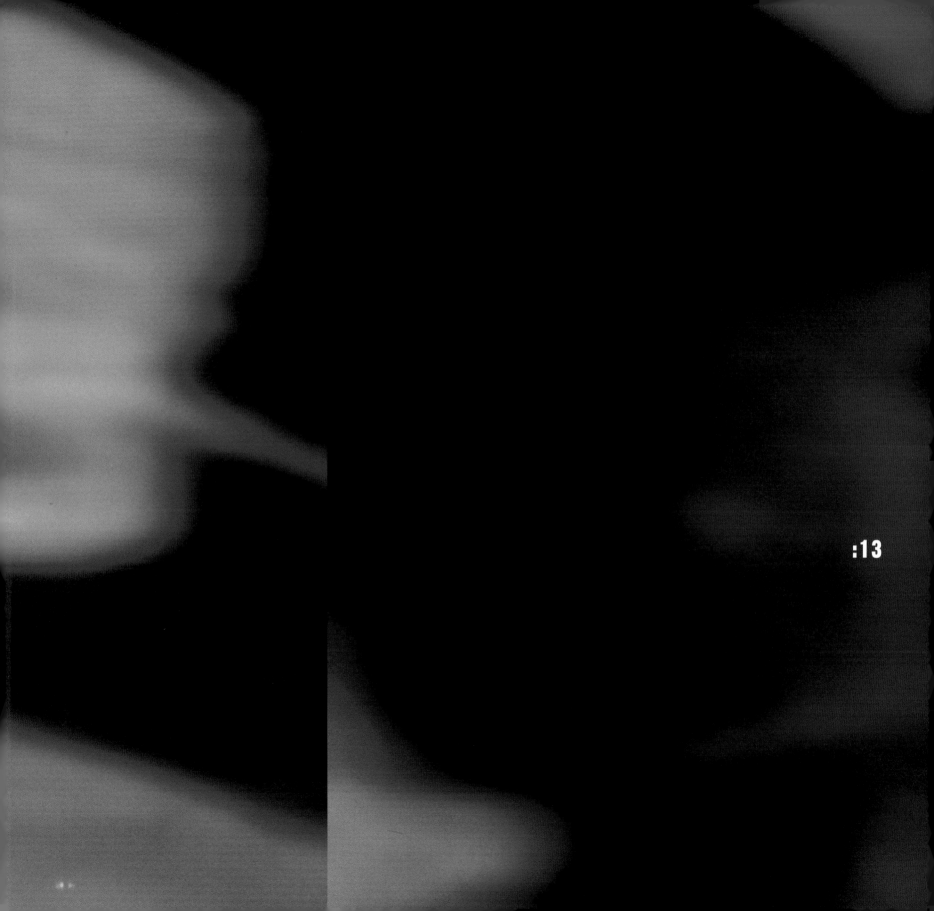

:13

steadi cam

shoot.

director.

HOWARD GREENHALGH

/ /

10.58   3 levels

prep.   composite.

2.89.00   2.89.45

rewind.   pause.   one-light.

playback   0   2   4   5

input.   switcher.   edit.

bio.   Although his video career began quietly in 1989 with a low-profile entry for singer John Marshall, Howard Greenhalgh's easy-going personality, carefully constructed scripts, and well-composed visuals quickly led him to big budgets and big names, such as Suede, Elton John, Sting, Placebo, and the Pet Shop Boys.

"They came in and gave me an immaculate set with action men on it," he said, of "Go West," the first of six camp extravaganzas he did with the Pet Shop Boys. "They're an art form in themselves. Are they a band or are they a painting?"

Along the way, Greenhalgh developed 1) a reputation for using maps, stars, and hands (long since abandoned) and for multi-layering (or, as he defines it, "slapping lots of bits on top of each other," also phased out); and 2) an affinity for technology.

That reputation, however, can be a double-edged sword. While readily admitting that digital manipulation is "a valuable string to my bow," he much prefers thinking of himself as a live-action director who can use computer graphics when necessary. "I'm constantly being asked for special effects, but I'm highly selective. It's a very expensive way to make something, and I don't want to be known purely for my computer graphics work," he says.

The Soundgarden "Black Hole Sun" video illustrates how well Greenhalgh's vision works, though, when harnessed to the right technology. The sophisticated computer effects underscore the song's "unsettling, sinister edge," not to mention Greenhalgh's bizarre take on "the residents of Happyland being sucked up to the sky by a black hole."

And although the video is a perennial favorite, Greenhalgh lost one battle over it. "I thought it would be amusing to have the band with those idiot grins, because they never ever smile. But in the end they wouldn't go for it."

Greenhalgh has been associated with two design and video companies, Why Not Associates and Why Not Films, which he co-founded well over a decade ago. He has been directing lucrative and award-winning commercials and been sniffing around features for some time now, but even after directing more than one hundred videos, he still loves the genre.

"I don't think I'll ever grow out of them . . . I love making them because I love the music, I suppose. When I was younger, I wanted to be a pop star. Maybe this is the next best thing."

BLACK HOLE SUN

SOUNDGARDEN   1994

PLACEBO

BRUISE PRISTINE
1996

"Howard is one of the jewels of the industry. His scripts are so well written and he understands how to use technology.
I would liken him to a world-renowned conductor who knows just what to bring in and when, whether it's a special effect or whatever."
– Ian Bird, computer animator

>> *DAYLIGHT FADING*
COUNTING CROWS

1997

0:01:27

AGE**8**HEARD**SINATRA**

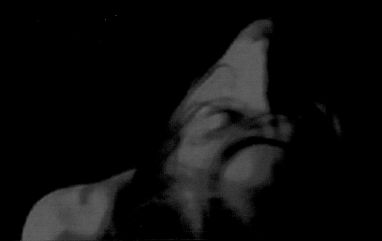

WILD AMERICA
<<
PAULA GREIF: IGGY POP   1993

bio.   In the mid 1980s, Paula Greif and co-director Peter Kagan caught people's eyes with their video for Steve Winwood's "Higher Love" and their spots for Barney's, where she had once been the art director. It was a harbinger of things to come from them, both together and separately. It was all the encouragement, for instance, Greif needed to segue from a distinguished career in graphic design to directing full time.

Her editorial and fashion pedigree is impeccable, including an education at the School of Visual Arts, three years as an art director at *Mademoiselle,* and a stint as the art director for the Richard Avedon studio. That sort of background infuses and distinguishes her video work, including the trilogy of public-service announcements for MTV's anti-censorship "Rock the Vote" campaign featuring Aerosmith, Lenny Kravitz, DEE-Lite, and Madonna (in the famous pose in which she is draped in an American flag). Those spots, along with another award-winning public-service anti-smoking campaign and her Esprit ads asking American youth what they would do to change the world, clearly reflect her editorial perspective. Her music videos for artists such as Billy Joel, Keith Richards, Ziggy Marley, Suzanne Vega, and, in particular, Iggy Pop in "Wild America" show what

can happen when a classical print sensibility is given a chance to tackle onto the screen.

Kagan also comes to video through fashion, although in his case as a photographer. After photographing runway shows on video, he decided to shoot a four-minute Super-8 fashion-oriented film. Completed in 1984 for $400, its gritty, black-and-white, crude look seemed perfect for music video. Greif showed the film to Jeff Ayeroff, who liked the intersection of fashion and music and gave them "a steady stream of work."

Kagan approached the videos more as an extension of the liner notes and as a chance to supply additional information about the song. "I never want to cast Layla," he says. "Let me imagine her forever."

After "Higher Love," in 1987, things were different. Video had changed the way television looked. "Advertising agencies began to see the coolness of this rougher, hand-held, faster-cut film attitude. They saw their beer bottles and cars in the midst of all the dancing, and I began to take big assignments from them. The innocence was pretty much gone from that point on."

director.	PAULA GREIF & PETER KAGAN	001 non-linear.			b/w	positive	0 2 4 5
			/ /		stylist.	dolly move.	on-line.	switcher.

director. **MICHAEL HAUSSMAN**

luminance.   640 x 480.

split   casting

hair & makeup.

<<   TAKE A BOW
MADONNA

1994

bio.   Michael Haussman began his film career at the University of Colorado, where he made the documentary film, *Shadow Sign,* which was nominated for an Academy Award. With that sort of momentum, he spent the next few years making experimental films, such as *Abandon 58,* which premiered at the Berlin Film Festival. Shortly thereafter, he made the jump to videos and commercials. He quickly distinguished himself with commercials for Levi's 501 Jeans, Adidas, Replay, Dockers, and the Guiness Enigma campaign. Based on Salvador Dali's paintings, the Enigma spots are now included as a permanent part of the late artist's perpetually traveling exhibition. His videos have been greeted with the same kind of enthusiasm. Although he worked with Chris Isaak, Paula Abdul, Bonnie Raitt, and Joe Cocker, among others, he is best known for his video with Madonna, "Take a Bow." That video not only won the MTV Video of the Year, but the prestigious Museum of Modern Art Award as well.

LEAVING LAS VEGAS
SHERYL CROW
1994   >>   hi-contrast   /
                                         treatment.

bio.   When David Hogan started doing videos in 1980, he was one of literally a handful of directors working in this country. Since there were no production companies, he actually produced his first fifty videos in his garage.

At the time, he saw it as a natural extension of his training as an artist. Born in Memphis, Tennessee, Hogan attended the Memphis Academy of Arts, where he studied painting, sculpture, and photography. In 1979, after a ten-year stint as an art director, he moved to Los Angeles, where he specialized in album cover and poster art.

The videos came soon thereafter. Since then, he has written and directed more than three hundred music videos, often distinguished by his skillful composition and love of saturated color, for artists such as Rod Stewart, Sheryl Crow, Joe Cocker, Steve Miller, Melissa Etheridge, the pre-symbol Prince, and Shania Twain.

In addition to being one of the only directors from the early era to profess music videos as his favorite art form and to still be working in the genre, he is one of the few directors to work not only in rock and r&b, but also in country. According to David Fincher, he was also the first music video director to use fashion models in videos. While not always hailed in some quarters as a positive development, it helped forge the connection between music and fashion, both in terms of fashion marketing and music programming, as well as, needless to say, between the musicians and models themselves.

director.   **DAVID HOGAN**   dailies.   8.35   style   clone.   casting.

YOU'RE STILL THE ONE
ᐱ **SHANIA TWAIN**
1997

/ influence: /   >>   *"There has been considerable progress in representations of women in rock video since MTV's*
inception. Time was — in the early '80s — all you ever saw were women in bathing suits in cages.
Nowadays, you're much more likely to see women in bathing suits in or near bodies of water."
– Mim Udovitch, "The Girlie Show," Rolling Stone, *October 14, 1993*

STEVE MILLER BAND   *YA YA*   1988   >>

0 : 01 : 35

director: | PAUL HUNTER | set | on | 0.01
composite: | off-line: | slo mo.

bio.   Having worked with artists such as Marilyn Manson, Puffy Combs, Lauryn Hill, Lenny Kravitz, and the Notorious B.I.G., Paul Hunter is one of the few directors who moves easily between rock and hip hop. A native Californian, Hunter majored in radio, TV, and film at Cal State Northridge and began his career working on film sets and doing commercials on spec.

Hunter became a director when a friend gave him five hundred dollars to shoot his video. The friend got a bargain, since Hunter went on to win Director of the Year at the Billboard Music Video Awards, two Maximum Vision Awards, and the Best Hard Rock/Metal Clip Award, as well as two MVPA awards, for Marilyn Manson's "Dope Show." The equally popular video for Notorious B.I.G.'s "Hypnotize" helped set the stage for Hunter's end-of-the-century assault on the airwaves, as Hunter unleashed a staggering barrage of videos.

The blitz, which harkened back to the early days of video, started with Will Smith's "Wild, Wild West," and continued unabated with Jennifer Lopez's "If You Had My Love," Lenny Kravitz's "American Woman," Enrique Iglesias's "Bailamos," T.L.C.'s "Upretty," Celine Dion's "I Want You to Need Me," and D'Angelo's "Untitled."

Hunter's ability to juggle so many assignments can be attributed to not just his focus but his unfailing habit of immersing himself in the video. "I was a big-time daydreamer as a kid, and I was good in photography. My first photography class [was] in ninth grade . . . I would get stuck in the dark room and miss two or three classes. It's kind of the same now. I get into something and I wake up in an editing bay and it's the next day."

As far as juggling so many different artists goes, that comes down to a combination of projecting a calm aura, telling a good story, and empathizing with the musician. "I like to feel that the work captures the intensity of the music," he says. "I become like the 'star' in a way; I'm secretly fantasizing I'm the singer. I put myself in their shoes, and imagine how I would like to be seen, and that's where I start."

/ influence. /   >>

"I enjoy the medium," Hunter told journalist Katherine Turman
in the August 1999 edition of SOMA *magazine.*
"Music keeps you at the pulse of the youth, which I love,
and I would like to experiment with it as long as I can."

<table>
<tr><td>Λ</td><td>ERYKAH BADU</td><td>ON AND ON
1997</td><td>MARILYN MANSON</td><td>THE DOPE SHOW
1998</td><td>>></td></tr>
</table>

WILD HORSES
U2
1992   >>   **U2**   *ONE*   *1992*   >>

lines per resolution.   720 x 486   choreography.

bio.   Phil Joanou has only directed a handful of videos, but has certainly chosen well: five with U2, two with Tom Petty, and a few more with B.B. King, Bon Jovi, and Whitney Houston and Mariah Carey. With clients like that, he doesn't need a formal bio to solicit work or to secure his position in the industry.

It's not that he would mind having a bio. As he wrote in response to having one, "If you would like me to write something more like . . . Phil Joanou attended USC's film school where he made the award winning film, *Last Chance Dance* . . . etc. etc. etc. I will, but I usually try to avoid it. But on the other hand, if this kind of write up is the format of all your other director's bios, like I say, I'll make up something short and sweet. Let me know."

For the record, then, let it be known that Joanou got started when he was a child "fiddling around with my dad's super-8 camera, making short two to three minute films with friends. I think we finally broke that camera! I believe it was run over by a car. At that point, we graduated to super-8 sound filmmaking. I was originally interested in being an actor and this was my opportunity to star in my own movies. When I realized that I should not be starring in my own movies, I started recruiting more friends and we made more and more elaborate films through high school and college. [It culminated in] the forty-five minute epic take-off on Star Trek, entitled *Star Trek: The Musical Picture.* Yes, it was a musical."

No expense was spared on the set. With a bit of cardboard, Christmas lights, and spit, his parents' garage became the bridge of the USS *Enterprise.* Then USC called. And Stephen Speilberg, who had been impressed enough with *Last Chance Dance,* who offered him a chance to direct an episode of Amazing Stories on the strength of it. From there, U2 asked him to direct "Rattle and Hum," and provided his entry into a regrettably brief but no less impressive video career.

director. | **PHIL JOANOU** |

storyboards.

WALLS
TOM PETTY   *1996*   >>

IT'S OH SO QUIET

^ **BJÖRK**

1995

director: **SPIKE JONZE**   0.00   effect   02091967
split screen.   posterize.   job#:

bio.   Spike Jonze is the first true video hero. This is no hype. He exploded on the small screen seemingly out of nowhere in the mid-1990s with a string of videos including the Breeders' "Cannonball," Wax's "Hush," and M.C. 900 Foot Jesus's "If I Only Had a Brain," but he had already made his mark: first as a BMX, skateboard, and alternative-fashion photographer and then as cofounder of cult magazines such as *Homeboy* and *Dirt.*

It was with "Sabotage," the Beastie Boys video that spoofed the cop shows of his childhood, that Jonze became a pop icon. The video won numerous awards, including the 1994 Best Director, Best Video, and Best Breakthrough Video; the Gold Clio/Best Video; and MVPA Best Video and Best Director.

The awards and accolades for the stream of videos that followed would take the length of this biography. Suffice it to say that anyone familiar with pop culture would recognize the videos for Björk's "It's Oh So Quiet," Daft Punk's "Da Funk," Dinosaur Jr.'s "Feel the Pain," or Weezer's "Buddy Holly."

Jonze is notoriously impossible to interview — a recent cover story in *The Face,* marking the first time a video director has made the cover of a major international lifestyle magazine, was all about the trials and tribulations of trying to interview Spike. (For this book, however, he has provided an exclusive: If he is to be believed, he flunked out of medical school and went to study structural engineering under his father during the building of the Panama Canal. It is, he swears, the key to his success. This feat is even more amazing considering that the Canal was built in 1904–14, which was at least several years before Mr. Jonze's, a.k.a. Adam Spiegel's, birth.)

Be that as it may, he is an auteur even if his videos are recognizable less for a visual style than for their wit, their irony, their references, and their structure. "I look at the videos as short films," he says. "I always tried to make sure they have a beginning, a middle, and an end."

When the stories are as intelligent as Jonze's, that's all you really need. As a result, he remains among video's most flexible directors and knows how to make every kind of budget work to his advantage. The video for Puffy Combs's "Benjamin's Remix" allegedly had a seven-figure price tag; yet Jonze's video for Fatboy Slim's "You've Come a Long Way, Baby," was made for less than one thousand dollars (which included buying a second boom-box when the first was stolen).

More to the point, the Fatboy Slim video won MTV's Best Video Award, as well as a handful of others, at the same time Jonze was racking up Golden Globes, critical awards for Best Director, and an Academy Award nomination for Best Director for his feature film, *Being John Malkovich.* Jonze is one of the first directors to come to the music video form after growing up with it, so it seems very fitting that he would be the first video director to be so honored. As anyone who knows him will attest, a more deserving lad could not be found.

on cue   medium
lipsync.   hi-contrast.   shoot.

0:01:45

0:01:46

CALIFORNIA

^
^ WAX

1995

0:01:47

<< NOTORIOUS B.I.G.   SKY'S THE LIMIT   1997

<< BEASTIE BOYS   SABOTAGE   1994

/ influence. / >>

"The guys with the shades? Some of the Beastie Boys. The other guy? He took the picture, and did the video,
'Sabotage,' that inspired it. Now, after making some of the greatest pop clips ever, he's directed his first film.
It's great. He's a pretty nifty actor, photographer, skateboarder and prankster, too. Spike Jonze: we salute you."
– Cover story introduction, The Face, *January 2000*

bio. Dean Karr had two jobs that prepared him for a career in music videos. The first was photography. There's nothing unusual or unexpected about that. He's neither the first nor the last person to cut his video teeth behind a still camera. The second job was a bit more idiosyncratic. He spent five years in a Seattle graveyard, working as a cemetery employee. The experience, combined with his instinctive attraction to dark, erotic romanticism, has influenced both his still photography and his video work.

The cemetery "is where my morbid fascination expanded from just an average horror film buff to actually finding science interesting for the first time in my life. Access to the afterlife and post-mortem rituals is powerful stuff, especially when you have an imagination," he says.

A glance at his work leaves little doubt as to the existence of his imagination. His still photographs have been showcased on more than twenty-five album covers for artists such as Guns & Roses, Tool, Marilyn Manson, and Busta Rhymes. He remains passionate about still photography because "it gives me a greater sense of immediacy and intimacy. I'm in and I'm out."

Cinematic work, such as that in the videos, is a bit more demanding: "It is usually a labor of love, and involves a greater sense of collaboration with my crew." He also feels that videos are more like an exhibit or a book than a single still. Even so, in both cases, "you are putting your soul out there for the world to judge."

Karr's visual sense is so strong that it sometimes disguises the amount of time and research that he puts into discovering an artist's taste. For "Crash," for instance, he took Dave Matthews to a Judas Priest concert, partly to gauge Matthews's reaction. (For the record, Matthews enjoyed himself. "Heck," says Karr. "Who knew?")

The ideal situation, Karr continues, "is working with an artist who has hired me for all the right reasons, fully entrusting that my imaging will make them look like a million bucks and set them apart."

That makes an association with an artist like Matthews, for whom Karr has directed four videos, particularly exciting. For the most part, though, bands that Karr likes frequently have "absolutely no budget. Unfortunately, it takes a decent budget to be able to make a video that involves canoeing up the Amazon River in Venezuela for ten days, or cage-diving with great white sharks in Australia."

Still, Karr finds it difficult to complain. Especially when you consider his previous place of business, you have no trouble believing him when he says, "I have been very lucky."

run and gun style.

6.66 daily move.

telecine transfer.

on tape

final master.

director.

DEAN KARR

pause

CRASH INTO ME
DAVE MATTHEWS BAND
1996   >>

0:01:52

MARILYN MANSON

SWEET DREAMS (ARE MADE OF THIS)

1995

/ influence, /   >>   *"Music videos: where art & commerce do not collide."*
— Billy Poveda, President & Executive Producer, Oil Factory, Inc.

^
^
DAVE MATTHEWS BAND   **CRASH INTO ME**
                            1996

DON'T DRINK THE WATER

DAVE MATTHEWS BAND

1998

SOUL TO SQUEEZE
<< **RED HOT CHILI PEPPERS**
                              1993

COME AS YOU ARE
NIRVANA   >>
                1992

IN BLOOM
NIRVANA   >>
                1992

| 640 | video | | | 256 | 0 2 4 5 | | **KEVIN KERSLAKE** |
| treatment. | split screen. | | treatment. | lines per resolution. | color balance. | director. | |

bio. Director/cameraman Kevin Kerslake first picked up a Super-8 camera when he was twelve. He was determined to capture the drama of skiing, which was a preoccupation that lingered throughout his teenage years in Mammoth, California. Not surprisingly, given the combination of passion and opportunity, he decided to become a sports filmmaker.

Once he graduated from high school, Kerslake moved back to his birthplace, Los Angeles, to study filmmaking at Loyola Marymount College. Two days before his first assignment — a surfing competition he had photographed — was due, he discovered that the negative he shot was completely black. To create a new project and still be able to meet the deadline, he decided to throw out the rules and shoot what he wanted. The experience taught him to listen to his "inner voice" and experiment with what he calls his "kaleidoscopic approach to storytelling."

Fueled by that vision, Kerslake settled down long enough to earn his degree, and to see his 1985 *"P" Diddle* thesis win the Southern California regional division Best Experimental Film in the Student Academy Awards. After getting it aired on cable television, Kerslake received calls from several production houses and began to direct music videos.

He has worked in video and commercials ever since and has thrived in the video world's willingness to allow him to explore "almost anything that tickles his creative fantasy." That love of exploration is evident in videos such as Mazzy Star's "Fade into You," and the Stone Temple Pilots' "Vasoline" and "Interstate Love Song"; as well as others for Green Day, k.d. lang, Filter, Smashing Pumpkins, Nirvana, and R.E.M.

That list is a testament to Kerslake's openness to alternative processes that transform color, contrast, texture, and focus; and to his ability to create "enigmatic and revealing imagery" through unusual casting, framing, and camera movement. It may be difficult to improve on his own description of his work: "promiscuousness with style."

INTERSTATE LOVE SONG   1994

STONE TEMPLE PILOTS

<<

FADE INTO YOU

MAZZY STAR

1994

>>

SIDEWINDER SLEEPS TONITE

R.E.M.

1992

/ influence. /   >>   *Pro-mis-cu-ity 1: a miscellaneous mixture or mingling of persons or things. 2: promiscuous sexual behavior.*
– Merriam Webster's Collegiate Dictionary, *Tenth Edition*

I NEED LOVE
SAM PHILLIPS   1994

0:01:61

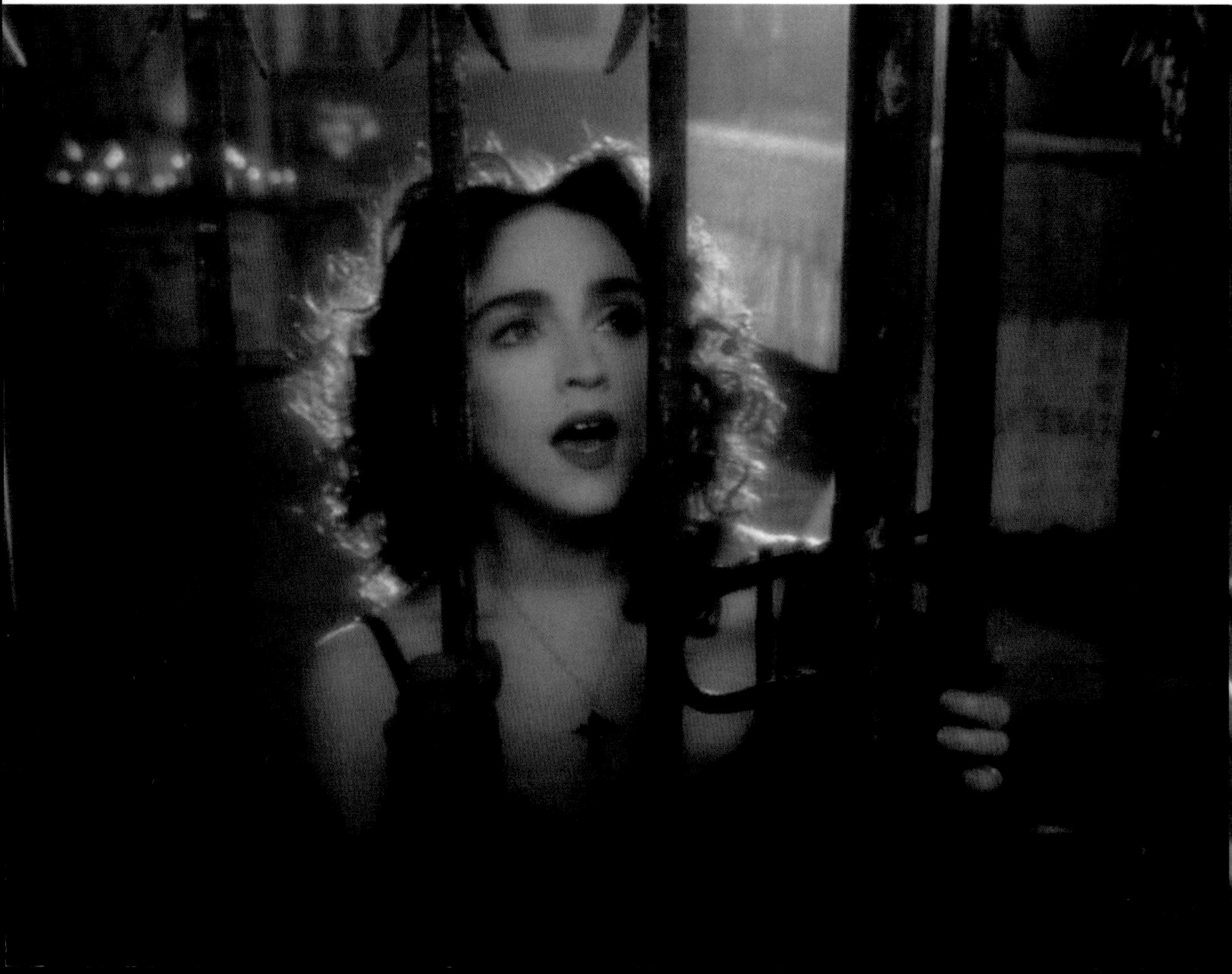

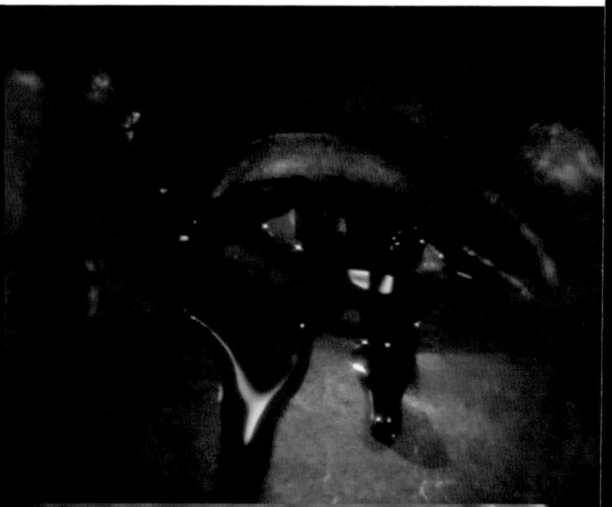

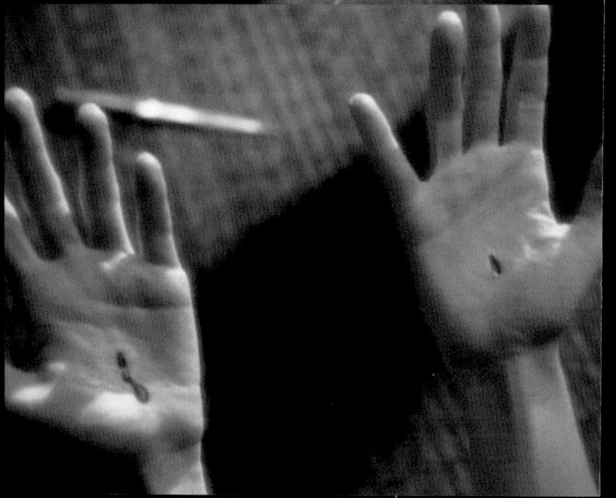

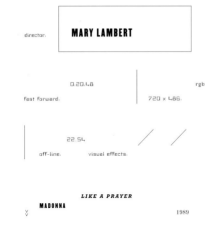

bia.   With videos such as Janet Jackson's "Control" and "Nasty Boys," and Madonna's "Like a Prayer," "Like a Virgin," "Borderline," and "Material Girl," Mary Lambert helped change the way we see not just video, but the world. Those videos remain so firmly imprinted in our minds that it is difficult to remember what it was like when a video such as "Like a Virgin" or, even more spectacularly, "Like a Prayer" had the power to ignite a social controversy that pitted generations against each other.

Lambert's videos had that power primarily because they were about something. Conventionally story-boarded and structured, the videos had a narrative flow and used Madonna not just as a singer and dancer, but as an actress as well. As a result, Lambert's early jump to features and television had a certain logic to it. Her first feature was the independent film *Siesta,* with Ellen Barkin, Gabriel Byrne, Jodie Foster, and Julian Sands. That led to television movies, episodes for the series *Tales from the Crypt,* and the hit film *Pet Sematary,* which was adapted from the Stephen King novel.

Lambert works regularly in Hollywood. Even though she does not do music videos anymore, her early videos, especially with the Material Girl, have given her a permanent place in music video history.

director.   **MARY LAMBERT**

0.20.48   rgb

fast forward.   720 x 486.

22.54.

off-line.   visual effects.

LIKE A PRAYER

MADONNA

V
V   1989

HUMAN BEINGS
SEAL   >>
        1998

director. **FRANCIS LAWRENCE**

1166   247   490   525   >>

daily move.   edit.

bio.   The son of a physics professor, Francis
Lawrence was born in Vienna, grew up in Southern
California, and was known for his natural curiosity
about how things worked. He went to college at
nearby Loyola Marymount University, where he made
the requisite short films and music videos and where
he forged an ongoing "symbiotic working relationship"
with Jeff Cutter, a fellow student and soon-to-be
director of photography. In addition to working as an
editor, both on his own videos and for other directors,
Lawrence directed twenty videos in 1999 alone, for
talents such as Lauryn Hill ("Turn Your Lights Down
Low"), Jennifer Lopez ("Waiting for Tonight"), Jay-Z
("Girl's Best Friend"), and Enrique Iglesias ("Rhythm
Divine"). The videos are marked by his adroit use of
post-production telecine and effects, as well as by his
high sense of style, especially in production design.

bright

luminance.   job#.

WHAT S SO DIFFERENT
GINUWINE
1999

0 : 01 : 65

0:01:66

director: **LESLIE LIBMAN & LARRY WILLIAMS**

YOU WIN AGAIN | LIVING ON THE EDGE OF THE NIGHT
<< **BEE GEES** | **IGGY POP** >>
1987 | **1989**

treatment.   storyboard   on-line:

bio.   Together and separately, Leslie Libman and the late Larry Williams have directed more than two hundred commercials and music videos. Since then, they have also directed major television episodes, series, and movies, such as *Homicide* (NBC), *Oz* (HBO), and *Out of Order* (MTV). Oddly, although the transition from video to television seems like a natural one, they are two of only a handful of video directors to work in television, rather than in advertising or features.

Libman came to music video via the cult film *Massacre at Central High School,* for which she served as assistant to the director. She then worked in production for the Robert Stigwood Film Company. While there, she was hired by record companies to write concepts for music videos. These concepts were so well received that soon she was producing and directing videos for artists such as Roy Orbison, k.d. lang, Rod Stewart, Suzanne Vega, and Belinda Carlisle.

Williams, on the other hand, came to video through photography. One of the original photographers to be exhibited at the Light Gallery in New York City, his work has appeared in museums from California to Paris and London and in magazines such as *Rolling Stone, Esquire, British Vogue,* the *London Sunday Times,* and *House and Garden.* He was on assignment for a magazine with Prince when the diminutive singer asked him to direct "When Doves Cry."

Although Libman and Williams continued to work as a team doing videos, their work in the mid- and late 1990s was increasingly in television. Their MTV series was called "as edgy and stylish as any post-modern music video. These stories deliver cautionary messages through moody mini-dramas. The *After School Special* was never like this." Their HBO drama, *Path of Paradise,* was singled out by *Time Out* for its "urgent camera work, twisted comic pathos," and stylish and compelling direction. And their production of *Brave New World* for Universal/NBC was widely praised for its "chilling evocation" of a world on the verge of amusing itself to death.

<<   **BUSH**   LITTLE THINGS   >>
1995

GOLD DUST WOMAN
∨ **HOLE**
∨   1996

director: | **MATT MAHURIN**

positive
e. c. u.   mHz.

bio.   Matt Mahurin has been a notoriously reclusive artist for years now. Back in the days when unlisted phone numbers were the exception, Mahurin, then a leading illustrator for magazines, was distinguished by not just an unlisted personal number but an unlisted business number as well.

That never stopped him from regularly winning design awards, or from appearing in underground magazines such as *Beach Culture* or high-profile ones such as *Time.* It was with *Time,* in fact, that he made perhaps his most famous/infamous statement. His manipulated photograph of O. J. Simpson, then on trial for murder, was an early example of the role technology plays in contemporary media. The cover image was altered to darken Simpson's skin tone and make his features more sinister, which was seen by many as racist. Despite the objections, the trend toward technological alteration has become more pronounced, and has caused artists such as David Hockney to abandon photography and return to painting, saying that painting is once again the most accurate representation of reality.

Regardless, Mahurin's experiments with pixelation and image manipulation and distortion anticipated the technological revolution by at least a decade. An unquestioned auteur, his vision has remained relatively constant. His recent video for Tom Waits, "Hold On," for instance, looks much like Bush's "Little Things" video and like the art he was producing in the late 1980s and early 1990s. In less skilled hands, that would be a criticism. To Mahurin's credit, the images have lost none of their freshness or their ability to jolt us into his alternative, gruesomely beautiful reality.

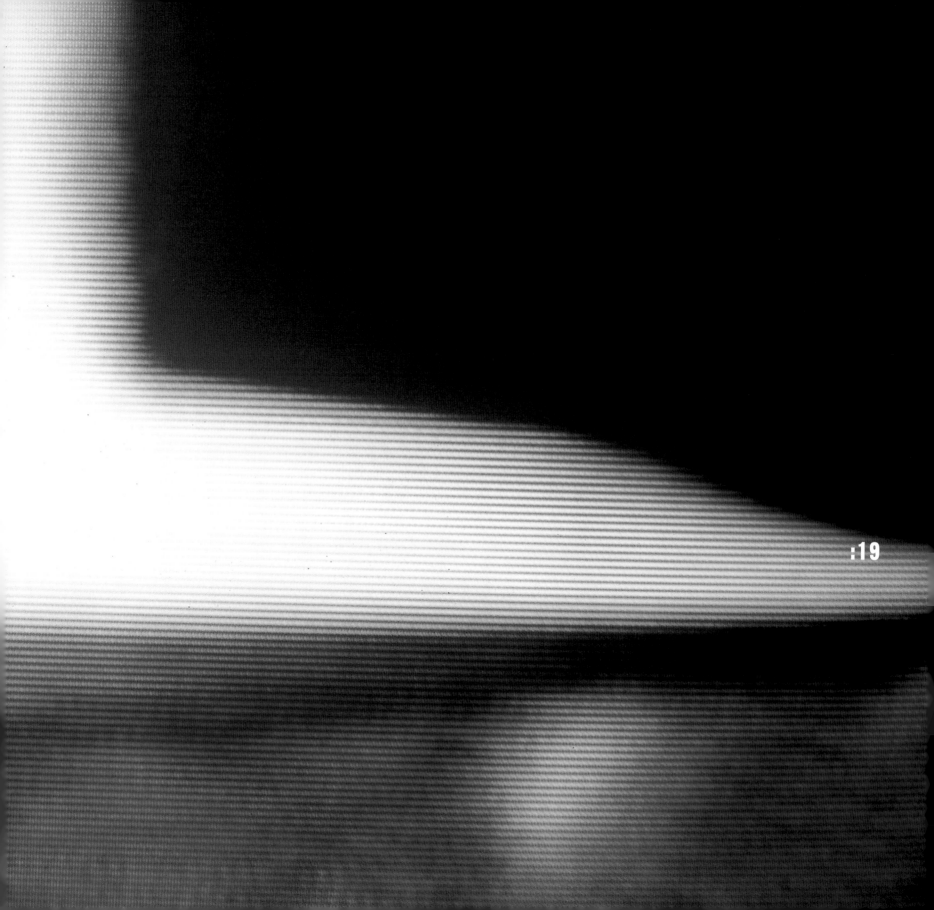

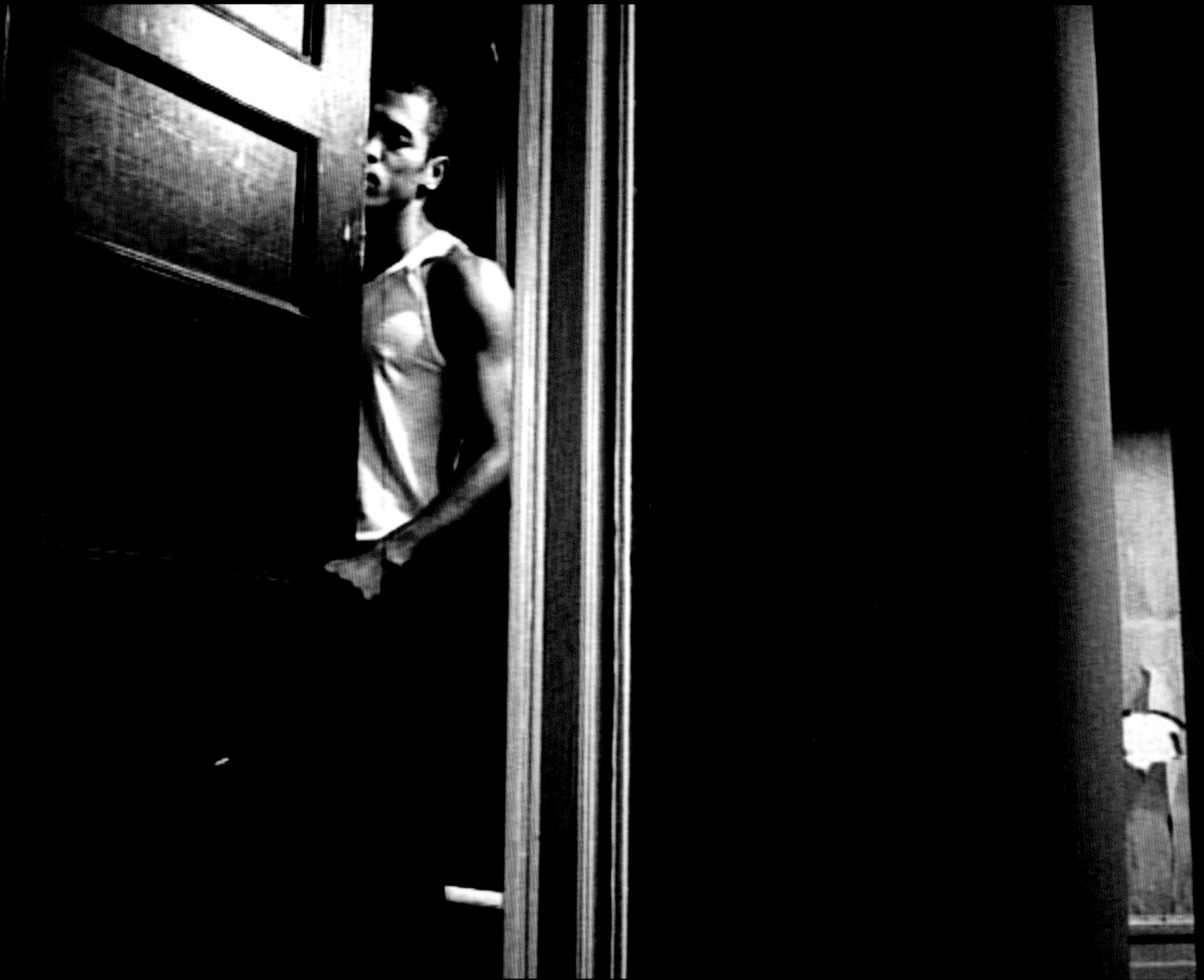

bio "I was born female, Jewish, and black, which has afforded me an unusual perspective on life," says Melodie McDaniel. "I am inspired by people who are socially outcast and I like to create spontaneous, 'real life' scenarios that highlight the subjects' stories into moving dramas or still lifes."

Given this inspiration, reinforced by a childhood steeped in social activism, lengthy stretches of time in an Israeli kibbutz, and a fierce insistence on continuing to confront "the reality of persecution and prejudice," it is not surprising that McDaniel's work is known for its depth, outstanding composition, and social commentary.

Her background may explain the rapport that Melodie McDaniel is able to establish with artists such as Madonna ("Secret"), Patti Smith ("Don't Smoke in Bed"), Annie Lennox ("Mama"), and even Perry Farrell (Porno for Pyros's "Cursed Female"). None of them are frivolous artists, and none of those songs are lightweight.

It would be a mistake, however, to characterize McDaniel primarily as a political artist, for the people in her videos, commercials, and still photography are never used for the larger statement at the expense of their individuality. It is by retaining their individuality and capturing their essence, in fact, that McDaniel is able to so effectively state her case. "Externals count a lot," she says. "Each person has a special meaning for me, something idiosyncratic in the shape of the head, nose, neck, whatever. I feel an intimacy when I work, a getting inside and then working it out."

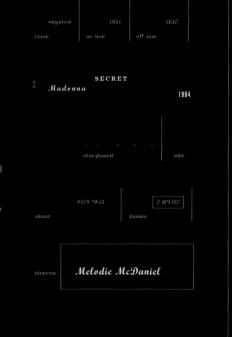

negative   001   002

clone.   on-line.   off-line.

SECRET
Madonna   1994

storyboard.   edit.

#69-9L0   2.89.07

shoot.   dailies

director   Melodie McDaniel

CURSED FEMALE

<< *Porno for Pyros*

1993

DON'T SMOKE IN BED

Patti Smith
1995

0:01:75

SIMPLE LESSONS

CANDLEBOX

1995

0:01:76

director:	**KEIR McFARLANE**		verify	final
			one-light:	production design:

bio: Australian director Keir McFarlane has a relatively unique approach to making music videos: "I suggest the most outrageous and radical idea I can think of, ask for the biggest budget I can get, pick up an MTV award, and soak up the success."

Realistically, however, that first idea "is rarely accepted. Most established artists, managers, and record companies have very specific ideas to contribute." In what can be a very political process, after "a couple of meetings they might accept a second, third, or fourth concept."

Surprisingly, some concepts emerge unscathed. "Initially," he says, "nobody liked the dark and disturbing short story I wrote for 'Mary Jane's Last Dance.' I suppose necrophilia isn't always an easy sell. But then a few weeks later Tom Petty called back and said the story kept haunting him."

Working with Petty, a bona fide star, and becoming part of "the MTV pop ideology is gratifying," he continues, but that experience is the exception rather than the rule. "Usually it is more interesting to collaborate with new artists who are willing to take risks."

McFarlane's videos, such as Candlebox's "Simple Lessons," the Wallflowers' "One Headlight," Sheryl Crow's "If It Makes You Happy," and Janet Jackson's "Anytime, Anyplace," demonstrate the latitude that successful artists often give to directors. Still, McFarlane, who has two videos in the Australian National Gallery collection, is critical of the current state of music videos.

"Music videos are an incredible opportunity for filmmakers to advance not just their careers, but the art form, which should be vital and ever-changing. There are now so many directors from film schools, art schools, and from the street that all music videos should be inspiring."

That, however, is not the case. "I'm sometimes disappointed to see directors churning out the same old clichés for the MTV factory. Unfortunately music videos are too much like commercials. Both are promotional devices intended to sell a product. Very occasionally a video exceeds its intention and becomes something more profound, like a political statement or even conceptual art."

McFarlane hopes the "anarchy of the Internet will soon break the monotonous stranglehold over the American music video culture and make it vital again." Until then, he feels his hands are tied. "Music video is pornography — you want to avert your eyes, but it is so fascinating. You can't rationalize it as art or your unique vision. It is a compromise that you make the most of creatively. Ultimately, the artists, managers and record companies have control. They own the product."

	edit	0	2	3		4		5
fast forward:	level:							

MARY JANE'S LAST DANCE
TOM PETTY & THE HEARTBREAKERS
1993

0:01:77

	BOYS OF SUMMER		IF THAT'S YOUR BOYFRIEND (HE WASN'T LAST NIGHT)	
<< DON HENLEY	1984	ME'SHELL NDEGÉOCELLO	1994	>>

director:	**JEAN-BAPTISTE MONDINO**

640 x 480	1.50	3 days	/ /
composite.	steadi cam.	shoot.	prep.

bio.   Photographer Jean-Baptiste Mondino helped bring fashion to MTV. His string of landmark videos — including Don Henley's "Boys of Summer," Madonna's "Open Your Heart," "Justify My Love," and "Human Nature," Sting's "Russians," and Bryan Ferry's "Slave to Love" — were among the best of the star-vehicle videos of the last fifteen years. Like his fashion photography, which pushed the trends toward color-saturated, offbeat, ironic, and sexual images as far as they could go, Mondino's videos have become iconic touchstones of an era.

Those videos worked, he says, because they were the last gasp of a mythology he does not believe exists anymore. "I was using the video to try to express what the song, the artist, was trying to say." But, he continues, things have changed rapidly in the past few years because of the rise of digital media and technologically based music. Although many photo editors, art directors, and the general public are reluctant to accept the implications of these changes, Mondino believes that the videos he did before, which emphasized the artist, are no longer representative of today's electronic zeitgeist.

"Music is the fastest expression of what is going on and I like that," he told *Lumiere* magazine. The changes, however, have made song-based music less interesting to him. "I love music that is like perfume sprayed into a room. Music that's just there. When you feel like you want to express a certain mood, you put on some techno, then some ambiance or maybe some house music. We don't even know who's making the music. It's just d.j.s mixing. There are no references."

Mondino finds the video form to be antithetical to the new music's anonymity. "That's why I'm not doing music video any more. Now the only thing I can do with music video is play looped sequences, the same way they do with this kind of music. They're still calling me to push an artist, but I love the idea that there are no more heroes. That's the massive difference between now and a couple of years ago."

Mondino has become so taken with technology that he's even moved away from conventional fashion photography, preferring instead to concentrate on technological manipulation. Given the quality of his music videos, his current disinterest in the form is a loss. Even so, his impression of what is happening remains as provocative as ever.

JUSTIFY MY LOVE
MADONNA
1990

/ influence. /   >>   *"The influence of music video has permeated pop culture, advertising,*
filmmakers, filmmaking technology, fashion, music . . . and even radio."
— Joseph Uliano, Executive Producer, Crash Films

HUMAN NATURE
MADONNA
1995   >>

director.

SOPHIE MULLER

prep   720 x 486

stylist.   crane shot.

rgb.

VENUS AS A BOY

<< **BJÖRK**

1993

0.08   edit

luminance.   clone.

bio.   Sophie Muller gravitated toward film while a graphic design student. Her master's thesis, a film called *In Excelsis Dio,* for the Royal College of Art made the festival circuit, won the J. Walter Thompson Prize for creativity, and helped her land her first "real" job: as third assistant director on the horror film *Company of Wolves.*

Since it led to more work, the B-movie served its purpose as a training ground. Then a childhood friend introduced her to John Stewart and Billy Poveda of Oil Factory Films, and her dream of becoming a director in her own right was realized.

From the outset, with the video for the Eurythmics' "I Need a Man," her skill was apparent. So was her passion, which explains why she remains that rare holdout from the lure of advertising. "I feel passionately about what I do. I have to feel passionate if it's going to be good. I like to be part of something, helping the music that I like to be successful. That's why I haven't done commercials. I can't imagine feeling the same way about a product. It's one step down the line to a bad thing, selling stuff that people don't want or need."

Interestingly, Muller is also one of the few directors to continue to stress the importance of performance in her video. "I'm not interested in concepts. I don't have them. I don't have ideas," she told the industry magazine *Promo* in 1997. Although that seems a distinctly idiosyncratic statement from someone as established as Muller, the simple fact is she remains fascinated by watching someone sing a song.

Take someone, for instance, like Annie Lennox, with whom Muller has worked repeatedly, including in the award-winning "Why." "Some people react brilliantly to a camera. When the camera is on Annie, something very interesting happens to her. She doesn't need much to put across the song."

The *Los Angeles Times* reacted similarly to Muller's video for No Doubt's "Live at the Tragic Kingdom." In a review of the video, Mike Boehm comments on her gimmick-free approach. Speaking of Gwen Stefani, he writes, "It's her face that makes her a star — both for its beauty, and her ability to mug like Lucille Ball, or to look like a tragically winsome old-time leading lady."

The review, which essentially used the video to promote the band's music, did not mention Muller by name. Other directors would have been upset. Muller, one suspects, simply viewed it as a job well done.

/ influence /   >>

"Muller's intrigue of 'theatricality and the sense of performance' grew out of a love of classic Hollywood musicals, and she cites The Sound of Music *as one of her favorite movies. 'I enjoyed the emotional impact of music when it came into a film,' she says. 'When I do videos now, I think of them as a musical interlude in a film.'"*
– Deborah Russell, Billboard, *January 1993*

<<   **ANNIE LENNOX**   WHY   1992   ∨∨

0 : 01 : 85

PINK

AEROSMITH

1997

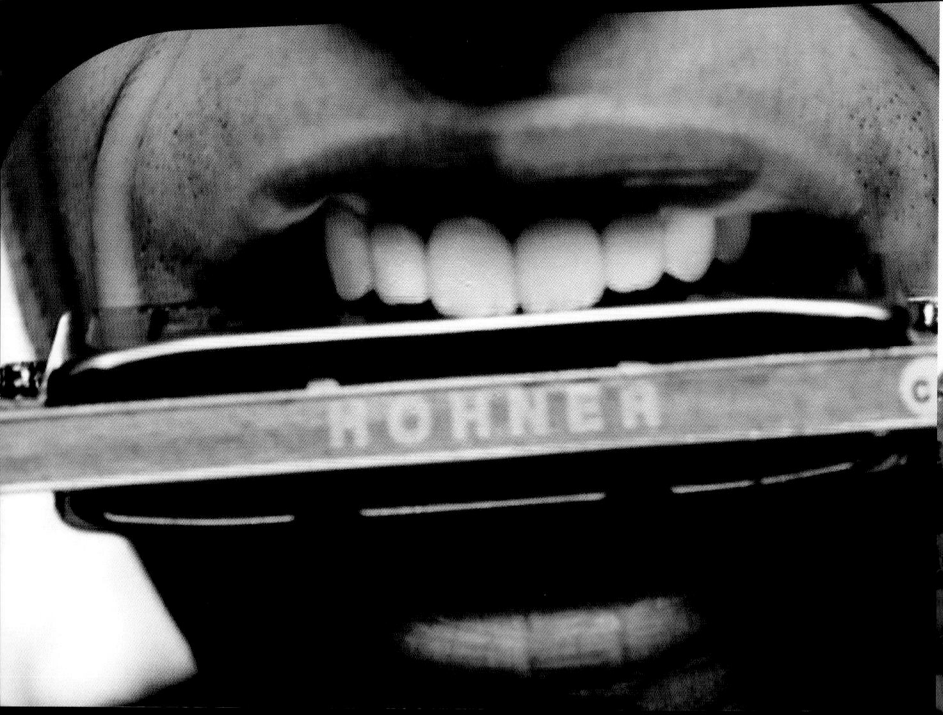

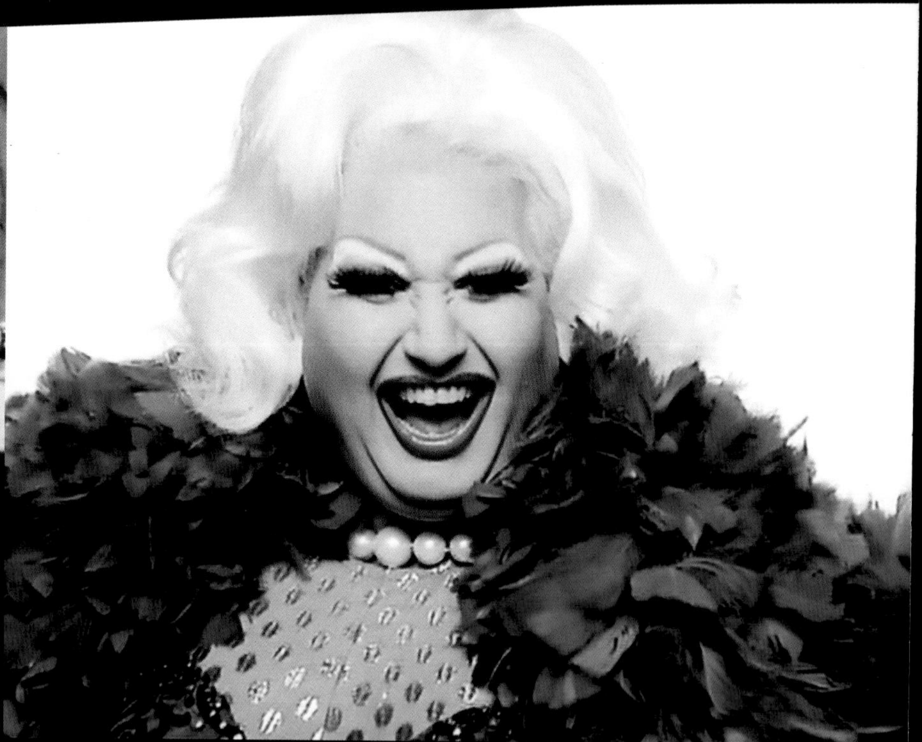

Doug Nichol was born in Los Angeles and studied film at the University of Southern California's Film School. While still at school, he worked on several Steven Spielberg films as a documentary cameraman. Upon graduation, he formed a production company with some classmates and started shooting and directing music videos and documentaries.

That experience led to a string of high-profile assignments, such as his long-form video of Sting's *Ten Summoners' Tales,* which won a Grammy Award in 1994, a feature-length film on Lenny Kravitz's world tour, and director of photography credits for Madonna's *Truth or Dare* movie.

Now living in London and Paris, Nichol has also directed more than fifty music videos, such as "This Is Hardcore," for the influential group, Pulp, "Mi Chico Latino" for the spicy Geri Halliwell, and "Mystical Machine Gun" for the hippie/reactionary band Kula Shaker. His most famous video is probably "Pink," which he did for Aerosmith in 1997, and for which he took home MTV's Best Video Award.

THIS IS HARDCORE
∨
∨ **PULP**
1998

director: **MARCUS NISPEL**

☐ format   ☐ insert

bio.   Marcus Nispel was born in Germany but found his way to America via a Fulbright scholarship in 1984, when he was twenty. Moving naturally from a foothold in advertising, where he was an art director for Young & Rubicam, he directed his first video in 1989. It was also the first video for C&C Music Factory. Although shot in what now seems like a prehistoric era, the video, "Gonna Make You Sweat (Everybody Dance Now)," remains a classic, and recently was listed at no. 74 in the *TV Guide*/ MTV "100 Greatest Videos of All Time."

While in New York, Nispel founded and operated his own production company, Portfolio Artists Network, but soon merged with the Scotts (Ridley, Tony, and Jake) to form RSA-USA and its video division, Black Dog Films. Since then, he has made more than six hundred commercials and videos and has become one of the most honored of all video directors.

Nispel's music videos, for example, include more than fifteen no. 1 songs and breakthrough videos for artists such as the Spice Girls, Simply Red, Puff Daddy, Bush, No Doubt, Cher, LL Cool J, Nina Hagen, the B-52s, Soul II Soul, Amy Grant, and the Gypsy Kings. He has been nominated for twelve MTV Video Awards, and won 1993's Best European Video Award for George Michael's "Killer/Papa Was a Rolling Stone." His work has been selected to be a part of the permanent collection at the Museum of Modern Art, and he was honored in the Film Society of Lincoln Center's "Cross Cultural Dreams Retrospective" with a retrospective of his music videos. He was also a recipient of the Black Achievement Award for the positive portrayal of African-Americans in mass media.

01.987   2.89   positive

white balance.   preroll.   e.c.u.

☐ format

MHz.   MHz.

GREEDY FLY
∧
∧   **BUSH**   1996

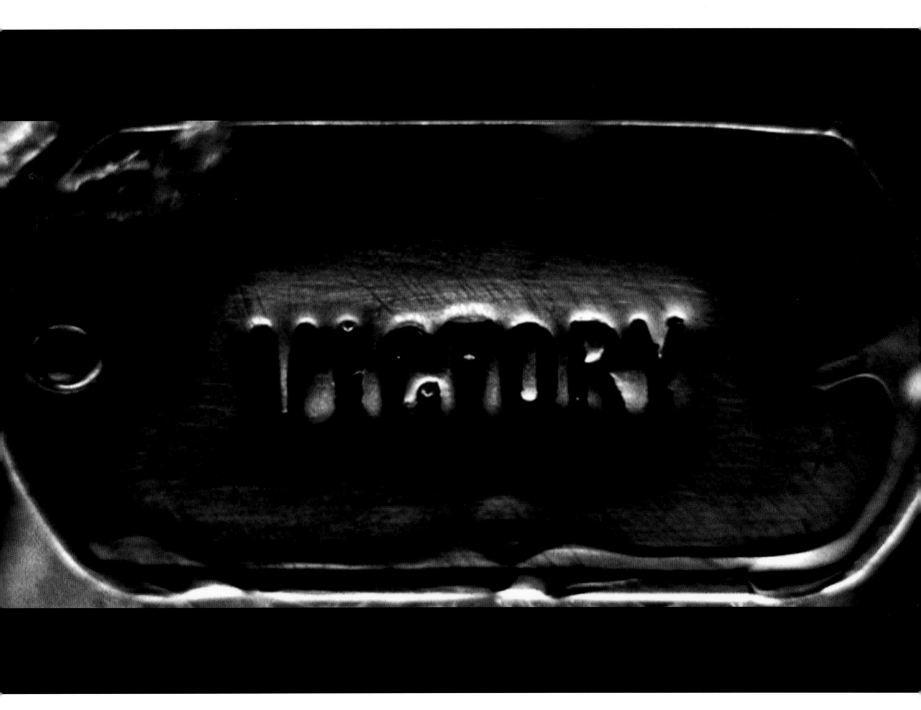

VICTORY
PUFF DADDY
1997

0:01:89

READY OR NOT

THE FUGEES   1996   >>

SPIDERWEBS

<<   **NO DOUBT**   1995

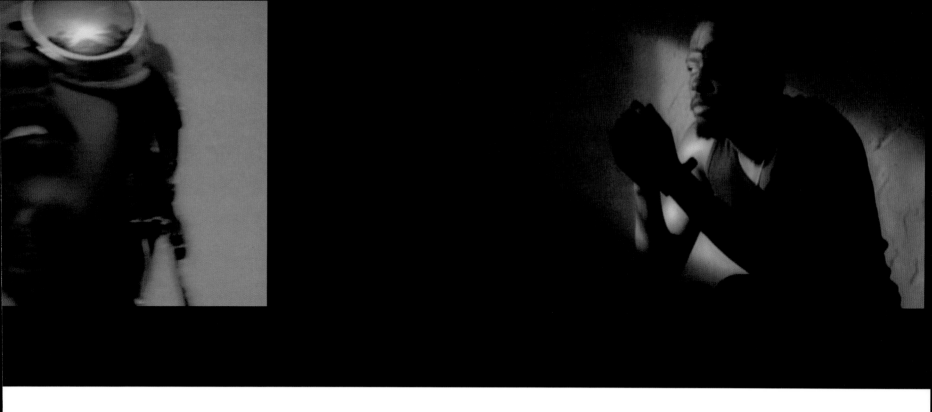

"Commercial art is the great art of the 20th century."
— Jim Czarnecki, Creative Director & Executive Producer, RSA/Black Dog Films USA - NY

director. **MARK PELLINGTON**

13	33	
treatment.	storyboards.	rgb.

JEREMY
<< **PEARL JAM** 1992 >>

bio.   Mark Pellington is probably the only director in the field to boast a degree in rhetoric. As predicted by his schooling, his videos are distinguished by a love of concept and a synergistic ability to blend live-action footage with found sound and images into effective aural and visual collages.

That ability has been evident from the outset. Straight out of school, Pellington got a job in the innovative On-Air Promotions Department of MTV. He quickly parlayed that experience into freelance directorial assignments for musicians such as Information Society, Malcolm McLaren, and De La Soul, and into text-image pieces with famed New York artist Jenny Holzer.

These projects led to his idea for "a non-linear collage program" called *Buzz*. Created in partnership with MTV Europe and commissioned by MTV and Channel 4 in the U.K., the thirteen-part global series was hailed by critics. The show generated, for the lack of a better word, a buzz for Pellington, propelled him out of MTV, and enabled him to become a director full time.

He did not waste much time, making an indelible mark early on with "Jeremy." The video, made for Pearl Jam, a band notoriously ambivalent about music videos, is a pitch-perfect encapsulation of the song's message and remains a perennial favorite on MTV and video "Best of" lists. Among its numerous honors are Best Director from the Billboard Music Awards and four MTV Video Music Awards, including Best Director and Video of the Year.

Pellington, however, was just getting started. Videos such as the Grammy-nominated INXS's "Beautiful Girls," Spearhead's "Positive," P.M. Dawn's "Set Adrift on Memory Bliss," Public Enemy's "Shut 'Em Down," and U2's "One" made him one of video's most sought-after directors. His video for the Jungle Brothers, "I Get a Kick Out of You," was chosen to appear with work from Wim Wenders, Jim Jarmusch, and Jonathan Demme in the AIDS-benefit special, *Red, Hot, and Blue*. His multi-screen images for U2's Zoo Tour raised the bar for live-performance environments all across the world; and his PBS film, *Words in Your Face*, with performers such as John Leguizamo, KRS-One, and Henry Rollins, anticipated the trend toward the spoken word by several years. His chronicle of his father's Alzheimer's disease, *Father's Daze*, was screened at the Berlin, Montreal, and Rotterdam Film Festivals; and his five-part PBS series, *The United States of Poetry*, was an epic performance that preserves countless voices that would otherwise be lost.

Pellington was one of the second wave of video directors to also make the jump to features, following his indie debut, 1997's *Going All the Way*, with *Arlington Road*, a thriller starring Tim Robbins and Jeff Bridges. In the context of this book, however, it is the rage and passion of "Jeremy" that forever lingers in the mind.

309		video	
job #.	clone.		playback.

WE'RE IN THIS TOGETHER

NINE INCH NAILS

v

1999

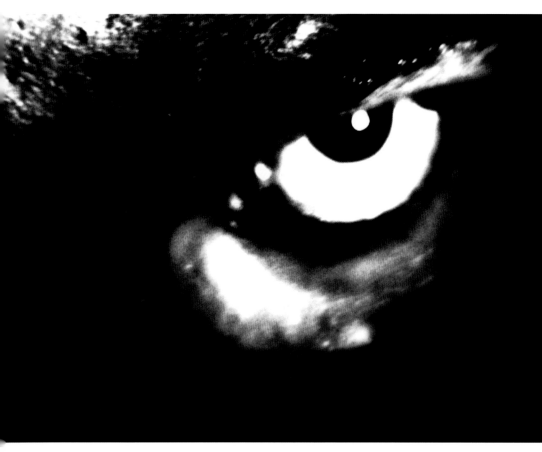

/ influence. /

>> *"Music videos are authentic expressions of a populist industrial society. For young people struggling to find a place in communities dotted with shopping malls but with few community centers, in an economy whose major product is information, music videos played to the search for identity and an improvised community."* — Pat Aufderheide, *"Music Videos: The Look of the Sound,"* Journal of Communication, *v. 36, 1986*

ONE (BUFFALO VERSION)

U2

1992

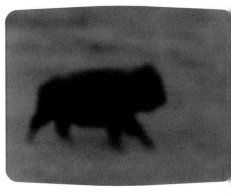

0:01:95

bio. Subversion is one of those values that is given lip service in the music world but is rarely achieved. Except in the work of Jeffrey Plansker, a director who has made a career out of biting the hand that feeds him.

The son of an advertising executive, Plansker grew up in Detroit infatuated with advertising. He attended his first shoot when he was two, and by the age of eleven he was editing his neighbors' home movies under the wing of his "company," Flying Glove Productions, named after a character in *Yellow Submarine*. College was the expected film-school route at Tufts University and at the School of the Museum of Fine Arts in Boston and, later, in the graduate film studies program at the School of the Art Institute of Chicago.

Although Plansker was appalled by advertising by then, he believed it was a fast track to a film career and proceeded to alternately dazzle and repulse the advertising world with a series of controversial commercials that incorporated radical graphic design elements, "frightening" soundtracks, and an almost brutal honesty.

These characteristics can also be seen in his music videos, such as the 10,000 Maniacs' "Candy Everybody Wants," which was based on a Noam Chomsky analysis of consumerism. "His work is playful and the song was playful," says Plansker, so he asked family friend and type-guru Ed Fella for the use of Fella's sketchbooks, which had type that resembled disfigured, melted chocolates. The video intertwined Fella's type, Plansker's twisted sloganeering (which he calls subtervising), and more typical images of Natalie Merchant. "I don't mean to confuse, but I find a certain joy in word collision and not necessarily feeling that it all make sense."

Plansker makes no secret that he prefers videos to advertising, but he is busy enough with other interests to prevent him from being prolific. He hosts two jazz radio programs in Los Angeles: one on Sunday morning, "Jazz Advance," and the other on Saturday night, called "Bohemia After Dark." Both feature the strong, hard-swinging jazz of the 1950s and 1960s of the Blue Note and Pacific Jazz labels, but, reflecting his view of art through collision, also make contemporary links with artists such as Kruder and Dorfmeister. He also is the founder of the cultural "cartel" Supply and Demand, which is responsible for a range of projects including CDs and an absurdist program in the tradition of Ernie Kovacs, who can still teach us a thing or two about subversion.

^ *MAHK JCHI*
ROBBIE ROBERTSON   1994

CANDY EVERYBODY WANTS
10,000 MANIACS   1992   >>

0 : 0 1 : 97

SPOONMAN

SOUNDGARDEN

1994

/ influence /   >>   *"To the 'filmmaker,' a chance to 'explore something creative.' To the 'musician' a mirror capable of instant replays."*
– Jeffrey Plansker

POSITIVE BLEEDING
URGE OVERKILL   1993   >>

<<

INXS

KISS THE DIRT

1986

ALL THIS TIME

1991

STING

>>

crane shot.

0

one-light.

output.

bio.   Alex Proyas was one of the first music video directors to make the jump from music videos to feature films. As a result, although his music video work generally took place in the 1980s and early 1990s and received little fanfare outside the music video world, his subsequent film work has helped establish music video's contribution to the look and feel of contemporary feature film.

Even at the beginning of his career, when the link between music video and feature film was tenuous, Proyas never had any doubt about his ultimate direction. While a teenager in film school in his native Australia, he made several short films, including *Strange Residues, Debris,* and *Groping.* All received critical attention, the latter winning Most Outstanding Short Film at the 1982 London International Film Festival.

The attention helped give him access to clients such as Coca-Cola, American Express, Nike, TDK, and Pepsi; and to musicians such as INXS, Fleetwood Mac, Sting, Crowded House, and Joe Jackson. As he was shooting those videos, he was also writing and directing his first feature, *Spirits of the Air, Gremlins of the Clouds,* which was completed in 1988.

Five years later, he released the gothic thriller, *The Crow,* which featured Brandon Lee (who infused the movie with a tragic history when he died on the set). Although greeted with disdain by many critics who resented the intrusion of the video-inspired look and editing styles (not to mention the volume of the soundtrack), the movie went on to earn nearly 200 million dollars at the box office. More to the point, its atmospheric look and high-volume soundtrack helped define the link between videos and features.

Proyas's video roots are still evident in his subsequent work, such as the controversial *Dark City.* While some critics were put off by the edginess of the vision, and the film was disappointing in terms of mainstream audience response, it was championed by other critics as an example of truly progressive moviemaking.

hi-contrast.　　　director.　　| HERB RITTS |　　r/g/b　　set　　final

color balance.　one-light.　rough cut.　　／　／　／　>>

LOVE WILL NEVER DO WITHOUT YOU

JANET JACKSON

1990

bio.   Leave it to Herb Ritts to make grit look beguiling. Besides Bruce Weber, perhaps no contemporary photographer has captured the strong, clean, graphic sensuality of the human form better than Ritts. His photographs, often in black and white, combine social history and fantasy in a way that has helped pave the way for the Abercrombie-ing of America.

Ritts has been pursuing this vision for more than twenty years, ever since he began photographing artists, athletes, political figures, actors, musicians, and models. His clients include companies such as Armani, Donna Karan, Calvin Klein, and the Gap. His museum shows have been crowd-pleasers everywhere from Tokyo to New York to Paris. His series of books (all proceeds from which go to charities such as AMFAR) remain in print. And his videos, particularly for Chris Isaak's "Wicked Game" and Janet Jackson's "Love Will Never Do Without You," demonstrate Ritts at his best: clean lines, strong forms, and a graphic simplicity that elevates his subjects to mythic stature.

CHERISH

MADONNA

1989

WICKED GAME
CHRIS ISAAK
1991

director. **MATTHEW ROLSTON**

rgb.   edit.

sdi   75i   100i

shoot   frame   video

dolly move.   composite.   clone.   on-line.

bio.   Matthew Rolston, one of the most influential still photographers of our time, has helped define the modern take on celebrity, fashion, and popular culture. For that reason alone, he was a natural for music video. The only question one could ask was what took him so long.

First he had to attend "nearly every art school in California" before enrolling at the Art Institute of San Francisco. There he discovered his affinity for photography and took off for an intensive three-year course at Pasadena's Art Center, College of Design.

While there, he started getting assignments from major national magazines. "I was impatient and had all the energy and drive that people have when they're starting out," he says. "I was also lucky."

He got luckier when he met Andy Warhol, who commissioned him to shoot Steven Spielberg for *Interview* magazine. It turned into a career launch. Over the years, his work has graced covers and pages of magazines such as *Harper's Bazaar, Vanity Fair, British Vogue, In Style, GQ,* and *Esquire.*

Because he understands the blurring of lines between marketing and image, advertising and entertainment, and style and substance, Rolston has been approached to do music videos that are meant to catalyze careers or imprint celebrity. That is something he has done repeatedly, be it for artists such as Janet Jackson ("Everytime"), Sheryl Crow ("There Goes the Neighborhood"), Garbage (whose letter to him regarding "I Think I'm Paranoid" is reprinted in the introduction of this book), Madonna ("The Power of Goodbye"), Matchbox 20 ("Real World"), or Bryan Adams (whose video for "The Only Thing That Looks Good On Me Is You" was nominated for a VH-1 Best Music Video Award). And although he has made a reputation for his glamorous approach, he can also hit a more emotional note, as in his video for Lenny Kravitz's "Thinking of You." In that video, he juxtaposed images of Kravitz against the backdrop of his mother, making the song, which is a homage to her, all the more poignant.

THINKING OF YOU

LENNY KRAVITZ   >>

1998

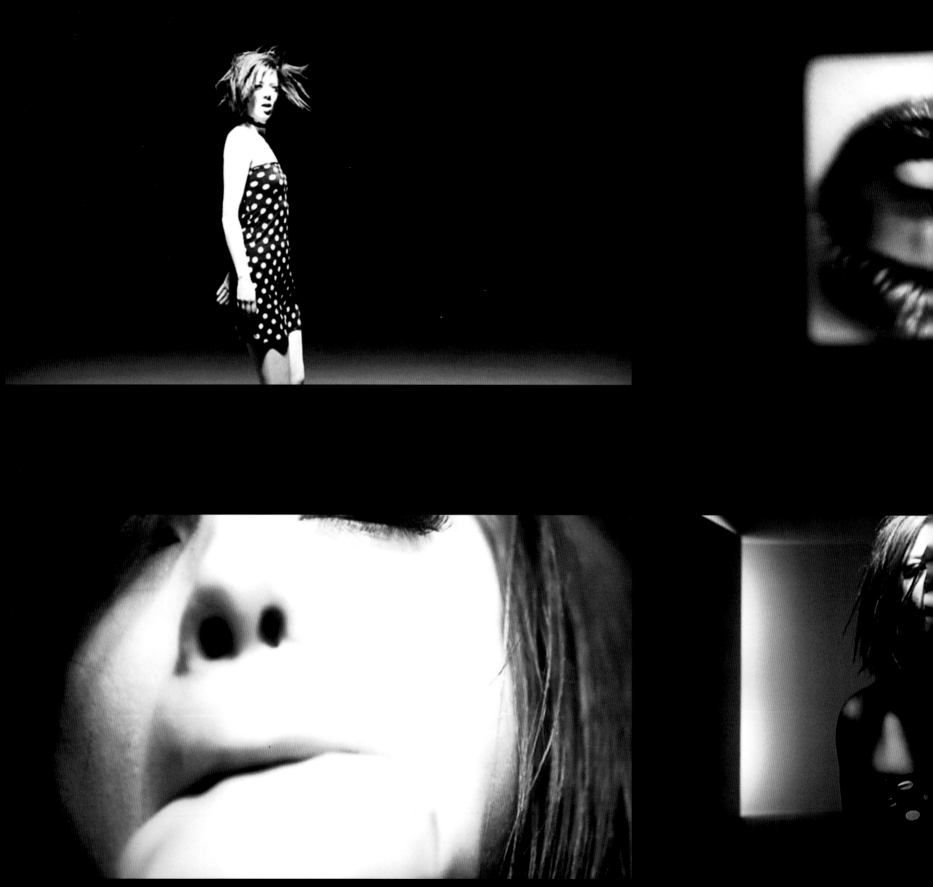

I THINK I'M PARANOID

 GARBAGE

1998

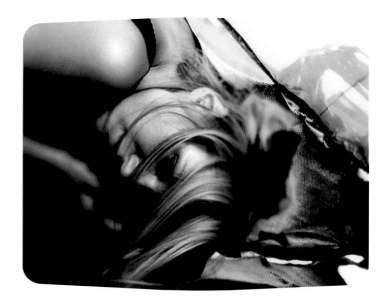

LONG HARD ROAD OUT OF HELL

MARILYN MANSON

<< 1997

FOOLISH GAMES

^ **JEWEL**

1997

0:02:11

0:02:12

<<   FIONA APPLE   CRIMINAL   1997

BECK   DEVIL'S HAIRCUT   1996

director.	**MARK ROMANEK**	edit		4.27.00	red		‖ ‖ ‖ ‖	stylist	video	0.00
		choreography.	rough cut.		color balance.	non-linear.		prep.	visual effects.	telecine transfer.

bio.   Few, if any, music video directors are as well respected as Mark Romanek. Whether it's directing the most expensive video of all time (the seven-million-dollar "Scream" with Michael and Janet Jackson), capturing an artist at the height of their visual power (Lenny Kravitz in "Are You Gonna Go My Way?" and En Vogue in "Free Your Mind"), reinterpreting familiar artists in a new way (Madonna in "Bedtime Story" and "Rain"), or pushing every known envelope (Nine Inch Nails in "Closer"), Romanek's signature on a video conveys an unmatched pedigree.

It is no accident, then, that MTV decided to acknowledge Romanek with it's Vanguard Video Award for lifetime achievement in 1997. As Janet Jackson said in her presentation speech, "the job of the music video director is not only to interpret songs but to create imagery that adds another layer to what the artist originally intended, often with images that leave a permanent impression on the viewer. This director possesses that gift — to represent music in a way that is unique, beautiful, haunting, and unforgettable. His videos lure you into a believable otherworld, where natural, supernatural, provocative, and surreal images exist and evoke a wide range of reactions, the same way dreams often leave you with feelings words just cannot describe."

Romanek has dabbled in features, with his 1985 independent film, *Static,* actually preceding his video career. He is unusual among video directors in that he sees videos as a tangent, rather than a prelude, to features. "Music video is like being a painter doing a series of sketches," he says. "Music video is like highlights in relief, like sculpting in time. The secret to a movie's success is its rhythm. Unlike a movie, a music video doesn't have to have narrative. And it's made to be seen on a small screen so you think about composition differently, like a miniaturist. It also exists in a flow of imagery, sandwiched between the VJs and garish programming, so you have to be graphically catchy. And if it becomes popular, you have to watch it over and over again. Because of that, you have to create from a different context than film, with hints and puzzles of narrative. You are drawn in by being told less, rather than more. If the narrative is a joke or too easy, you lose interest. Because I don't like videos that you understand the first time, all I need for it is pieces and nuances."

The "pieces and nuances" have allowed him to win more than a dozen MTV awards, a Grammy, three Clios, nine MVPA awards, and a place in the permanent collection of the Museum of Modern Art (with "Closer" and "Bedtime Story"). It is a record and a career he is justifiably proud of.

The only regret Romanek has, in fact, is that as a director, he doesn't own a single frame of the video. "If I make a music video a hit, if it makes it into heavy rotation and becomes entrenched in the culture, I still don't own it or stand a chance to reap anything from it. I don't like that at all."

NINE INCH NAILS   PERFECT DRUG   1997

LENNY KRAVITZ   IF YOU CAN'T SAY NO   1998

Thirty Frames Per Second

NINE INCH NAILS

CLOSER

1994

BEDTIME STORIES

MADONNA 1995 ˅

:24

director. **ROCKY SCHENCK**

start   video   now

playback.   on-line.   off-line.

/   //

NICK CAVE & KYLIE MINOGUE

WHERE THE WILD ROSES GROW

1995   >>

bio.   Rocky Schenck is a video director distinguished by his liquid images, impressionist landscapes, and innovative lighting, which all harken back to his background as an experimental filmmaker and still photographer.

Born in Dripping Springs, Texas, Schenck grew up loving film. After attending art school, he moved to Los Angeles, where his photographic prowess and offbeat sense of humor attracted still photography and video work for artists such as P.J. Harvey, Seal, Joni Mitchell, Annie Lennox, Rod Stewart, the Cramps, and Alice in Chains.

Dedicated to pursuing excellence in all mediums, Schenck has made films that have been shown in numerous festivals, has written and staged plays, and has been a recipient of a grant from the American Film Institute. If there is any unifying theme to these endeavors, it is his use of a number of styles to express his personal mythology. Although water, death, isolation, and redemption are favorite themes, Schenck is also a true humorist. As such, he is never at a loss to present those themes as a reflection of life's ironic sweetness.

NEVER NEVER GONNA GIVE YOU UP

LISA STANSFIELD   1997

0:02:21

She's gone.

director: **JAKE SCOTT**

EVERYBODY HURTS
R.E.M.   1993

bio.   Jake Scott is one of a few video directors who has naturally struck a balance between his artistic and commercial sensibilities. His work includes two videos on *TV Guide* and MTV's end-of-the-century roster of the top 100 videos; and his contribution to the field also includes being co-founder of the respected video company Black Dog Films. Founded in the late 1980s, it has given talent such as Marcus Nispel and Chris Cunningham a home and has turned out influential videos for everyone from Madonna and No Doubt to Puff Daddy, Mariah Carey, and Janet Jackson.

Business notwithstanding, Scott is most interesting as a director. The two videos that were mentioned in the 100 greatest videos poll, Radiohead's "Fake Plastic Trees"

Silence is gray,

and R.E.M.'s "Everybody Hurts," are typical of Scott's style, which *Shoot* magazine characterized as "poetry in motion." As these videos illustrate, Scott is interested in capturing the "gamut of human emotion, embodying humor, pathos, and aesthetic wonder."

It is this sense of humanity that mirrors R.E.M.'s starkly harrowing "Everybody Hurts" and helps explain why the clip touched such a nerve. Ultimately it swept the 1995 MTV Video Awards (Best Director, Best Breakthrough Video, and two technical merits), won a MVPA Award, and was called "a seminal piece of film art" in *Artforum.*

That is the stuff careers are made of. As so many do, Scott made his way into commercials, for clients such as Acura, Nike, and RCA. His series of ads for RCA,

including the spots, "Bulldozer," "Sunrise," and "Feels Like," was honored by the Museum of Modern Art in 1997; and his work for Blaupunkt won a Bronze Lion at the Cannes Film Festival.

Although advertising and features beckon, Scott remains an advocate of music video, feeling it gives him more space to work with than commercials do. More recent videos include Tori Amos's "Past the Mission," which he shot in Spain; and two clips with k.d. lang, including the ethereal "Mind of Love." He also has won what is perhaps the silliest video award category of all with "New," a video featuring No Doubt from the *Go* soundtrack, which took home the 1999 VH-1 Vogue Fashion Award for Most Stylish Video.

LIGHTNING CRASHES

LIVE

1995

0:02:24

STARING AT THE SUN

U2   1997   >>

0:02:26

director: **STEPHANE SEDNAOUI**

25 frames

storyboard:

stylist:

3.58.24

clone

non-linear:

bio: Stephane Sednaoui is a French photographer who is equally known for his film work, having won MTV's Best Breakthrough Video award in 1992 for the Red Hot Chili Peppers' "Give It Away."

Although a relatively simple video, it is still fresh, perhaps because the video so perfectly mirrored the band, the song, and the times. The concept, which can be distilled down to the fascination of watching a band sweat off its metallic coat of body paint, posed some initial health concerns.

"At first, I was very worried that the band could stand the body painting in the desert heat for two days," he says. But the band was not really bothered by the climate or the generic location, which Sednaoui chose specifically because "there was nothing special about it."

The director was also worried about the band's ability to provide enough charisma in front of the camera, but there too it was worry for nothing. He was so impressed with lead singer Anthony Kiedis's "explosion of energy" on the first take that he realized that he didn't really need to provide a lot of coaxing to the band.

He has since done numerous videos, including U2's "Mysterious Ways," Fiona Apple's "Sleep to Dream," Madonna's "Fever," Alanis Morissette's "Ironic," and R.E.M.'s "Lotus." He has also continued to pursue his print career, contributing to magazines such as *Interview, Per Lui, Arena, Details, The Face, Vogue Hommes, Detour,* and the *New York Times Magazine;* and gaining acclaim for album covers for artists such as Madonna, P. M. Dawn, Chic, Grace Jones, and Mick Jagger. "Music has always inspired me," he says. "Even when I do photos, I get energized and inspired by the music." Although he has wanted to direct a movie since he was twelve, "I am not in a rush to direct a movie, but it will happen. I enjoy photography and videos so much. They are an important part of creating images of all kinds, no matter what the medium happens to be at any given time."

FEVER
MADONNA

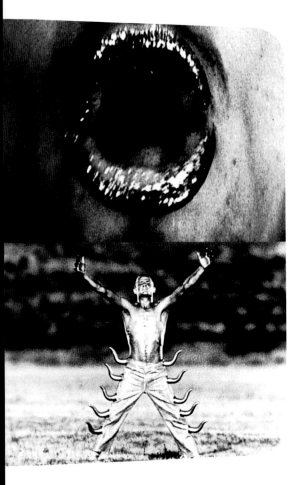

GIVE IT AWAY
MIXED BIZNESS

RED HOT CHILI PEPPERS   1991   **BECK**   2000

<<   >>

TIN MACHINE   *ONE SHOT*   1991   BLUE NILE   *HEADLIGHTS ON THE PARADE*   1990   JANET JACKSON   *IF*   1993

director. **DOMINIC SENA**   non-linear   split screen.   prep.   a.   b.   c   10.28.00   rough cut.

bio.   One of the founders of Propaganda Films, former cameraman Dominic Sena made his mark on video history with a series of high-profile videos. Some of these were for prestige singers such as Anita Baker ("Talk to Me"), Blue Nile ("Headlights on the Parade"), and Sting (the haunting "They Dance Alone"). Many more were for dancing divas, such as Tina Turner ("I Don't Want to Lose You"), Jody Watley ("Don't You Want Me"), and Janet Jackson. His videos for Jackson, including "Miss You Much," "If," and "Rhythm Nation," not only helped make her a superstar, but broadened the appeal of hip-hop dancing as well.

Sena directed more than one hundred music videos during the 1980s alone and was awarded various cinematography awards during that time, including the Eastman Kodak Certificate of Visual Excellence. In the last ten years, he has concentrated primarily on commercials and features. Three of Sena's spots, Nike's "Bouncing TV" and "Dueling TVs" and Apple's "Coal Train," helped earn Propaganda the Palme d'Or at the 1992 International Advertising Festival in Cannes. The Nike campaign also won Sena a Gold Lion for Individual Achievement.

He is perhaps best known for *Kalifornia,* his feature film debut. Starring Brad Pitt, Juliette Lewis, and David Duchovny, it, like the films of Quentin Tarantino, was viewed as an announcement of the new independents' invasion of Hollywood.

78.92   casting   #28   a   2   4   5

freeze frame.   switcher.   shoot.   choreography.

bio.   Floria Sigismondi, who leaped to the forefront of the music video avant-garde with her early videos, combines an array of disciplines, including painting, sculpture, design, photography, and film, into a style best described as intense. She pulls theatrical and dramatic imagery from Italian opera and Greek mythology, saturates it with color, and then builds what she calls "entropic underworlds inhabited by tortured souls and omnipotent beings" that arise from her "scandalous subconscious."

It may be that she's just living up to her name, Floria. Her parents, who were opera singers, named her after a character in the opera, *Tosca*. When she was two years old, her family emigrated from Pescaia, Italy, to Canada. Her formative years were divided between this creative, unconventional European family of artists and the rigid conformity of an all-girls' Catholic school in the industrial town of Hamilton, Ontario.

In 1987, Sigismondi moved to Toronto to study painting and illustration at the Ontario College of Art. As soon as she was exposed to it, though, photography became her first love. By the time she graduated, she already had a full fashion portfolio.

Although she was immediately successful as a print photographer, Sigismondi soon moved on to music video. Her vision attracted artists such as Marilyn Manson and David Bowie, and comparisons to masters such as David Lynch and Federico Fellini. What with shots of Manson shaving his armpit ("Tourniquet") or having his mouth pushed open by a dental device or rows of marching boots ("The Beautiful People"), the videos justify the kudos.

While some critics have objected to the darkness of Sigismondi's images, most recognize the intelligence behind her approach. Rather than try to shock people, she says, she is only "looking for beauty in darkness, to make some kind of harmony in the images."

director.   **FLORIA SIGISMONDI**

visual effects.   job#.   6906   hi-contrast.   shoot

on-line.   off-line.   1 3 5   113   >>

lines per resolution.   edit.

TOURNIQUET

<<   MARILYN MANSON   >>

1997

0:02:34

0:02:36

TRICKY   MAKES ME WANNA DIE   1997

0:02:37

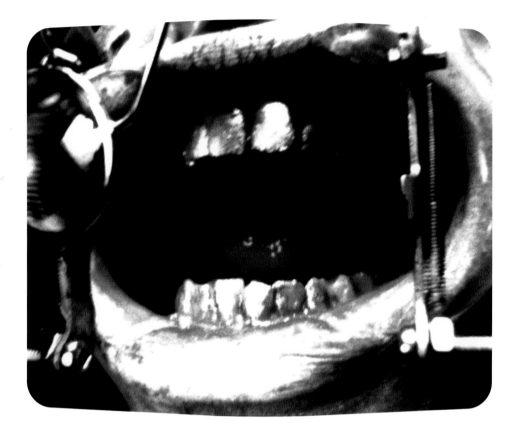

THE BEAUTIFUL PEOPLE

<< MARILYN MANSON 1996 >>

0:02:39

<< **PRODIGY**
BREATHE
1997

| **THE VERVE**
BITTER SWEET SYMPHONY
1997 >>

crane shot.   lipsync.   pause.   0.05   0.00   hi-contrast   one-light.   640 x 480.   director.   **WALTER STERN**

bio.   Walter Stern, who has been directing music videos since 1990, has become closely identified with the trend toward darker, more disturbing videos. This reputation began with his association with Prodigy, which spans from the band's days as an underground collective to its international stardom.

The videos for "Firestarter" and "Breathe" not only helped break the band but established Stern as a video director of note as well. Both videos had one-day shooting schedules. "Firestarter" was easier, primarily because it was more improvised and did not involve working with an alligator, which only "moves when it wants, according to temperature." In "Breathe," the band had to occupy a living, breathing house. To accentuate the weirdness of the house, Stern edited the video in filmic, rather than "promo," terms: "It cuts against the grain, not on the beat, which I think just leads you to stop noticing the track. The intention was to build a climax visually."

The Verve's "Bittersweet Symphony" could have been a retreat to normalcy for Stern, but ended up being equally disturbing. In this one, the singer, Richard Ashcroft, deliberately and unsympathetically antagonizes people so that the viewer is happy that he gets beaten up. In the director's cut, Stern ends with a shot of the singer's face drenched in blood. The band vetoed the shot, saying it was too much like acting and that it would ruin their chances of getting the video onto all but the most adult television shows.

Stern was much happier with "Teardrop," a video for Massive Attack that features a fetus floating in amniotic fluid (not a real fetus, given the risk of electrocution, but a realistic one nonetheless). It puts comments he made about "Bitter Sweet Symphony" in a new light. "It's been compromised," he said about that video at the time. "The whole idea was to push boundaries, make things more adult." It's ironic that he makes that happen by returning to a womb.

director.	**JOSH TAFT**		04987	2.89		positive		/ /
		white balance.	preroll.	e. c. u.	mHz.			

bio.   As befitting his Seattle base, Josh Taft's earliest success was with bands of the emerging grunge scene. Although he has broadened his base since then, he still enjoys a reputation for spotting and breaking new bands via video.

"That's my moniker," he says. "New bands can be much better to work with because they are actually excited and have as much enthusiasm as you do. You feed on that, and end up making a better video."

Taft begins with the song. "I try to find out what its essence is, and then express what and how it makes me feel." For the video of Stone Temple Pilots' "Lady Picture Show," for example, Taft wanted to play with the idea of early cinema.

The song singled out women. "Because I wanted a representation of that era which was innocent and true to the context and technology of the time, I researched historical stock footage and pulled twenty to thirty shots from the girlie shows of the 1920s," he says. "I kept a low-tech approach and got the visual effects without electronics. I used the color break (of an otherwise black-and-white video) to break the expectation, and kept the images innocent so that the video would be fun without being exploitive."

His take on "Award Song" for a Tribe Called Quest illustrates his related preference for something "simple and uncluttered. I didn't want to use a stupid story or tricks that often mark hip-hop videos; and I used a gold frame in particular to show that some things can be just as beautiful as a classical painting."

The frame had another purpose, too. "I never liked the way television frames an image, and I'm aware of how different things look from one TV to another. So I wanted to redefine the frame and vary the relationship of the picture to the frame. I've seen the video in different situations, on different television sets, and it holds up."

OCEANS

PEARL JAM

1992

0:02:43

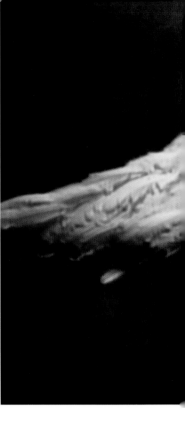

LOSING MY RELIGION
<< R.E.M. >>
1991

SWEET LULLABY
DEEP FOREST
1993

ᵛ

director. | TARSEM | 00.98 | | luminance. | job# | prep.

3.58

dailies. | 1 2 3 | non-linear.

0:02:44

rough cut

switcher.   tracking shot.

clone.

bio. A native of India, Tarsem Dhandwar Singh is the director who gave MTV a jolt with his video for R.E.M.'s 1991 smash, "Losing My Religion." It was one of those rare videos that not only took the song to an entirely new conceptual level but also broke all sorts of visual expectations for a video in heavy rotation on MTV. In addition to its unusual classical allusions to the Russian filmmaker Andrei Tarkovksy and the Italian painter Caravaggio, it was perhaps the frankest exploration of homoeroticism MTV had ever seen.

It was also a video where Tarsem lost more than his religion. "I was so nervous I kept going to the loo to throw up. My assistant thought I had a drug problem," he told *Rolling Stone* in its 1992 survey of "The 100 Best Videos of All Time."

Because "nothing freaks me out like doing a video," Tarsem has only directed a handful of videos, including the deeply personal "Sweet Lullaby," from a song by Deep Forest, that was filmed on several continents in one month. Although Tarsem works regularly all over the world, his work is mostly focused on commercials for clients such as Smirnoff, Nike, and Levi's Jeans and on the completion of his first feature film.

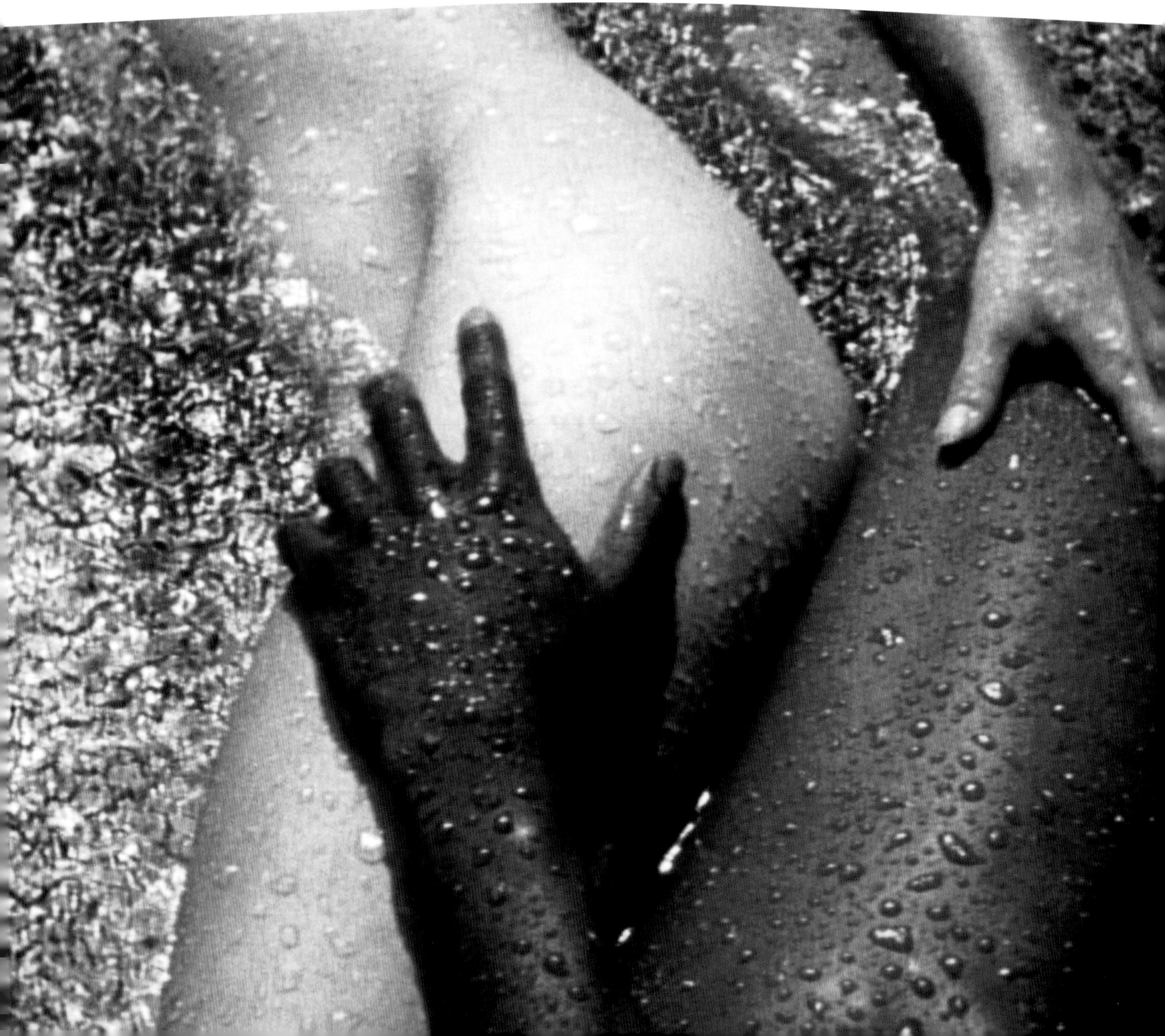

| director: | **PAULA WALKER** | | 6.37 | | set | |
| | | edit. | sio mo. | steadi cam. | | prep. |

bio.   Paula Walker was performing with dance troupes at fairs and on television in Los Angeles by the time she was six. After an injury ended her dance career, she studied theater and film at the University of Michigan and then returned to Los Angeles to pursue a career. She got a day job in television production, which financed her more creative short experimental films about the dance world.

These films brought her to the attention of Warner Bros. Records, who initially hired her to cast dancers and work out dance moves. Soon, however, the choreographer became a director. As far as she saw it, the progression was a natural one.

"Filmmaking is like dancing. You plot dynamics and movements in space. Try to get under the surface and capture a subliminal quality. Get rid of the clutter and create a mood or atmosphere. Lighting a film is like writing poetry. Filmmaking in any form is about memories, dreams, and desires," she says.

That explains why her videos are known more for their styling, locations, and sensuality than for their dancing. "A lot of my work involves creating movement out of everyday gestures and actions for nondancers," she told *Advertising Age* in May 1988.

Six years later, discussing her video for Tina Turner's "The Way of the World" in *Creativity* magazine, she explained the visceral and diffused visuals as a way to create "another time and place."

"The whole thing about filmmaking is that you're trying to get away from reality," she said. "You're trying to abstract it or dissect it or create an alternate one, so that people are seeing something different."

Walker rarely works in music video anymore, concentrating instead on feature film projects and commercials. Even so, she credits music video as "a way to experiment and have fun. It was a way of free-form experimentation. A lot of times, you experiment on a technique that will show up later on in your work. It's always a process of development."

Thirty Frames Per Second

THE NEVILLE BROTHERS

FEARLESS

1990

TALKIN' BOUT A REVOLUTION

∨ TRACY CHAPMAN

1989

SHE'S A BITCH

<< **MISSY ELLIOT** 1999 **TLC** NO SCRUBS 1999 >>

bio. Harold Williams, better known as Hype, grew up wanting to be a painter in New York, like Jean Michel Basquiat or Keith Haring. He didn't do much with oil but he managed to put hip-hop on a larger canvas: MTV. Quietly announcing a hip-hop franchise, Williams's Mad-Max inspired take on Tu-Pac's "California Love" upped the genre's stakes with its cross-over appeal and high production values. Before long, Williams was everywhere. However, it wasn't until the video for Missy Elliot's "The Rain (Supa Dupa Fly)" that Williams really broke.

The clip placed the full-figured Elliot in a patent-leather suit pumped full of air. When she found out his plan was to make her look like the Michelin Man, she was incredulous. "Trust me," he told her. "It's going to be hot."

It was. The video, with its surreal, distorted, saturated look and its company of dancers decked out in shiny yellow raincoats, helped make Missy Elliot a star and got Williams nominated for a Best Video on MTV. He outdid himself the next year with a variation of that style for the Busta Rhymes song, "Dangerous." Recently he broke out of hip-hop with a video for No Doubt's "My Ex-Girlfiend." He did not, needless to say, put Gwen Stefani in the Michelin Man suit.

director. **HYPE WILLIAMS**

4.02.00

shoot

treatment

hair & makeup.

freeze frame.

run and gun style.

WORD UP
<<   **MEL G.**

1999

OUT OF CONTROL
THE CHEMICAL BROTHERS   >>

1999

director.   **WIZ**

visual effects.

3.58

01   23   45   67

720 x 486.

split screen.

playback.

0:02:52

bio.   Wiz has been called a rave poet, but while his forte is dance music, his vibe is pure rock 'n' roll. A former musician, DJ, and photographer, Wiz is a self-described master of self-promotion. He is also fond of incorporating drug references like "uncut and undiluted imagery" into his work, as well as of a personal style that includes an exposed midriff, androgynous fashion, and an Apache hairdo.

To some that might be considered pandering, but Wiz is a genuine artist with a passionate commitment to music video. His videos are among the most sexual and the most hedonistic. *Weekender*, an eighteen-minute short film about the band Flowered Up and about the wilder side of dance-club culture, caused a sensation when it was aired in 1992 on Channel 4 in Britain, and it has been credited with launching the recent genre of British youth-culture movies such as *Trainspotting*.

Wiz's videos are extraordinary chronicles of an array of British underground superstars, such as the Happy Mondays, Suede, the Beloved, Manic Street Preachers, Ian Brown, and the Chemical Brothers, with an occasional Mel G. (Spice Girl) and Jamiroquai thrown in. Traditionally taking the position that he dislikes discussing his work, he described his career to *Promo* magazine in July 1999 with this admission: "Filmmaking is the art of regret. Moments of great ecstasy, followed by moments of great horror. I've had wonderfully exhilarating and personally fulfilling artistic achievements. And I've also suffered other times of crippling self-doubt." Since he calls the first chunk of his career "the Ecstasy period," that isn't particularly surprising.

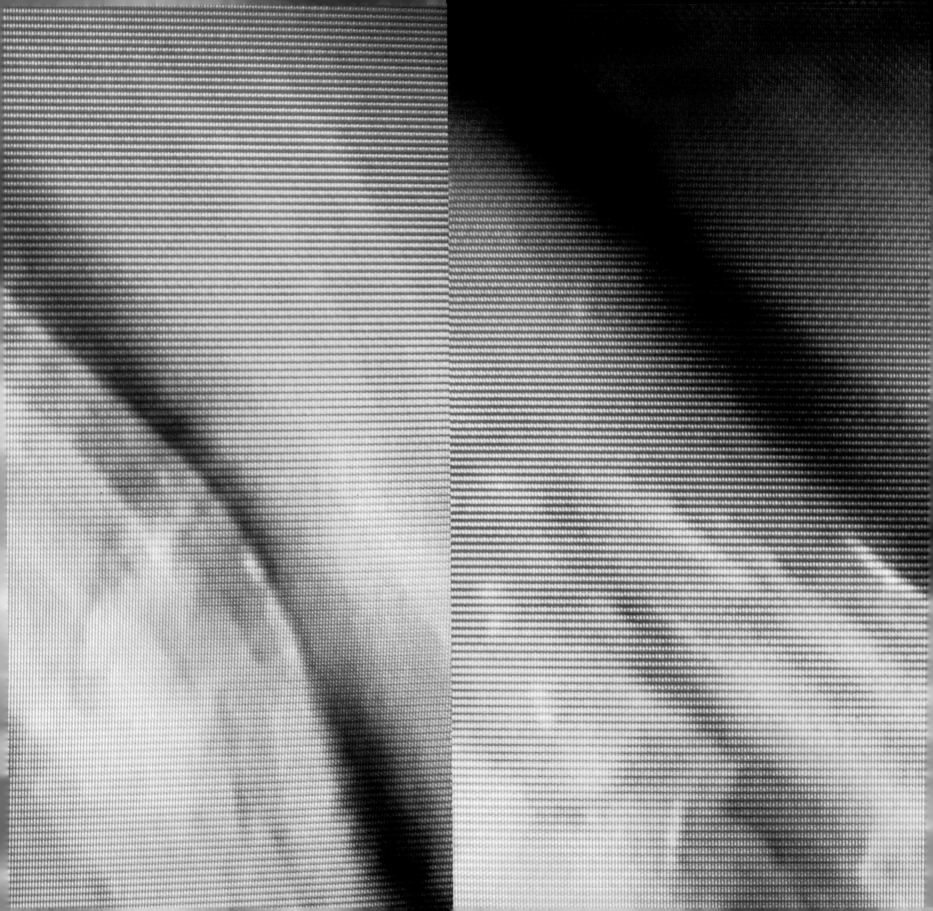

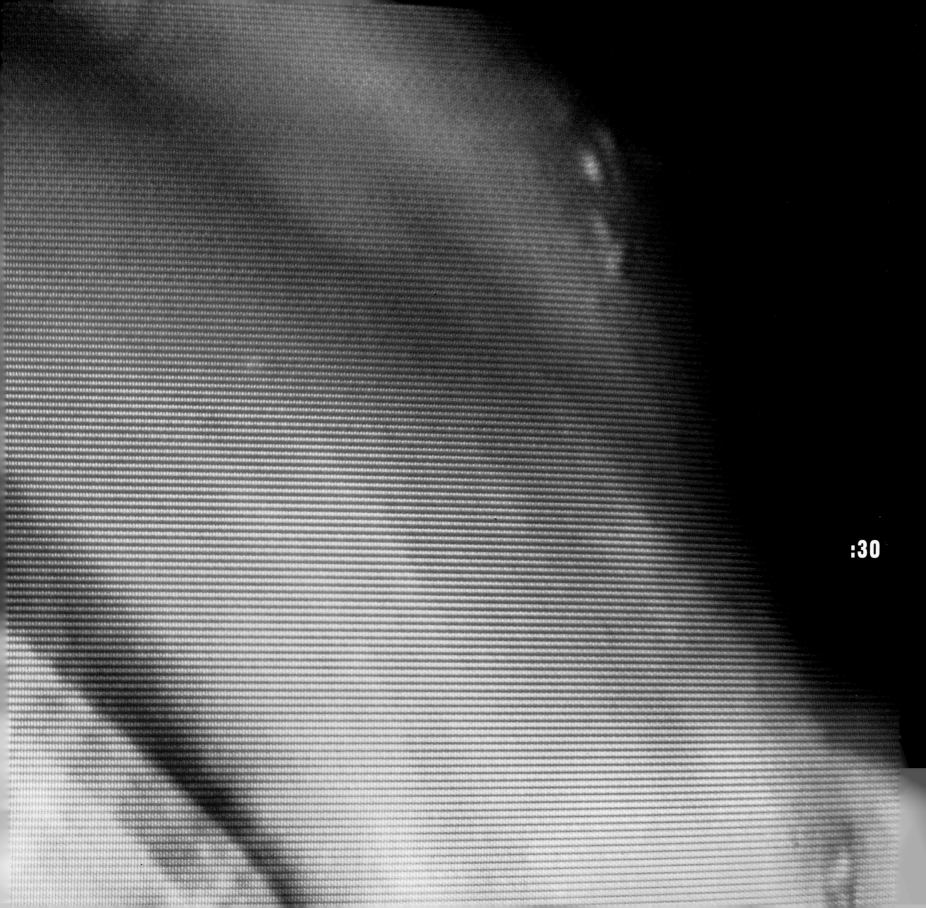

:30

SELECT VIDEOGRAPHIES

director. JONAS AKERLUND

video.

Stefan Anderson — Walk Right On
Marie Fredriksson — Mellan Sommar Och Host
Marie Fredriksson — Sa Lange Det Lyser Mitt Emot
    Anne Lie Ryde, Ah En San Karl
Per Gessle — Do You Wanna Be My Baby?
Per Gessle — Kix
Kajsa — Angel Eye
>> Madonna — Ray of Light
Meja — Rainbow
Moby — 007 Theme
>> Prodigy — Smack My Bitch Up
Roxette — Fingertips
Roxette — June Afternoon
Roxette — Run to You
Roxette — She Doesn't Live Here Anymore
Roxette — Una Dia Sin Ti
Roxette — Vulnerable
Izabella Scorupco — Shame
Sinclair — A la Ronde
Svante Turesson — Allt Borjar Nu
Whale — Pay for Me
Wilmer X — Destination

director. GEOFFREY BARISH

video.

Joan Armatrading — The Shooting Stage
Cowboy Junkies — Misguided Angel
Don Henley — Heart of the Matter
>> John Hiatt — Have a Little Faith
John Hiatt — Slow Turning
Chris Isaak — Don't Make Me Dream about You
>> Lenny Kravitz — Mr. Cab Driver
>> Spear of Destiny — Never Take Me Alive
Warren Zevon — Sentimental Hygiene

director. STEVE BARRON

video.

Adam and the Ants — Ant Music
Bryan Adams — Gonna Run to You
Bryan Adams — Heaven
Bryan Adams — There Will Never Be Another Night
Bryan Adams — This Time
a-ha — Crying in the Rain
a-ha — Crywolf
a-ha — Hunting High and Low
a-ha — Living Daylights
a-ha — Manhattan Skyline
>> a-ha — Take on Me
a-ha — The Sun Always Shines on TV
Joan Armatrading — Drop the Pilot/What
    Do Boys Dream
Joan Armatrading — Kind Words

The Bee Gees — ESP
David Bowie — As the World Falls
Eric Clapton — Tearing Us Apart
Natalie Cole — The Christmas Song
Natalie Cole — Unforgettable
Natalie Cole — When I Fall in Love
Culture Club — God Thank You Woman
Def Leppard — Let's Get Rocked
Dire Straits — Brother in Arms
Dire Straits — Calling Elvis
Dire Straits — Heavy Fuel
Dire Straits — Money for Nothing
Sheena Easton — Machinery/Ice out of Rain
Sheena Easton — Magic of Love
Sheena Easton — Telephone
Eddy Grant — Boys in the Hood
Eddy Grant — Frontline
Eddy Grant — Living on the Frontline
Eddy Grant — Till I Can't Take Love No More
Eddy Grant — I Don't Wannna Dance/Electric Avenue
Heart — Who Will You Run To
Heaven 17 — Let Me Go
Heaven 17 — Penthouse and Pavement
Don Henley — All She Wants to Do Is Dance
Human League — Don't You Want Me
Human League — Feeling Fascination
Human League — Louise
Human League — Love Action
Billy Idol — Sweet Sixteen
Joe Jackson — Real Men
Joe Jackson — Steppin' Out
>> Michael Jackson — Billie Jean
The Jam — Dreams of Children
The Jam — Going Underground
The Jam — Strange Town
The Jam — When You're Young
Lyle Lovett — Here I Am
Madonna — Burning Up
Paul McCartney — Pretty Little Head
OMD — We Love You
Dolly Parton — Potential New Boyfriend
The Pretenders — My Baby
Simple Minds — Glittering Prize
Simple Minds — Promised You a Miracle
Simple Minds — See the Light
Spandau Ballet — Life Line
Rod Stewart — Baby Jane
Styx — Haven't We Been Here Before
Supertramp — Better Days
Supertramp — Cannon Ball
Tears for Fears — Pale Shelter
Toto — Angel Don't Cry
Toto — Holyanna
Toto — Rosanna/Africa
Toto — Stranger in Town
Marshall Tucker Band — Silverado

Marshall Tucker Band — This Time I Believe
XTC — All of a Sudden
ZZ Top — Double Back
ZZ Top — Give It Up
ZZ Top — Rough Boys
ZZ Top — Sleeping Bag

SAMUEL BAYER

Afghan Whigs — Honky's Ladder
Bad Brains — God of Love
Blind Melon — No Rain
David Bowie — Hearts Filthy Lesson
David Bowie — Strangers When We Meet
Buffalo Tom — I'm Allowed
Cracker — I Hate My Generation
Cracker — Nothing to Believe In
The Cranberries — I Can't Be with You
The Cranberries — Ode to My Family
The Cranberries — Ridiculous Thoughts
The Cranberries — Zombie
>> Sheryl Crow — Home
Sheryl Crow — My Favorite Mistake
Melissa Etheridge — Come to My Window
Melissa Etheridge — If I Wanted To
Fishbone — Servitude
Fishbone — Unyielding Conditioning
Garbage — I'm Only Happy When It Rains
>> Garbage — Stupid Girl
Garbage — Vow
Hole — Doll Parts
John Lee Hooker — Chill Out
John Lee Hooker — This Is Hip
Natalie Imbruglia — Identify
The Jesus & Mary Chain — Far Gone and Out
Lenny Kravitz — Black Velveteen
LL Cool J — Father
Marilyn Manson — Rock Is Dead
John Mellencamp — Just Another Day
John Mellencamp — Your Life Is Now
Metallica — Until It Sleeps
>> Nirvana — Smells Like Teen Spirit
Offspring — Gotta Get Away
The Rolling Stones — Anybody Seen My Baby
>> The Rolling Stones — Saint of Me
>> Smashing Pumpkins — Bullet with Butterfly Wings
Suicidal Tendencies — Nobody Hears
The The — I Saw the Light
Urge Overkill — The Break
Robbie Williams — Angels

BIG TV!
(ANDY DELANEY & MONTY WHITEBLOOM)

Paula Abdul — Will You Marry Me
Paula Abdul — Blowing Kisses in the Wind
Paula Abdul — Promise of a New Day
Bananarama — Love Truth and Honesty
Beloved — Deliver Me
Beloved — Hello
Beloved — Only Your Love
Beloved — Satellite
Beloved — Sweet Harmony
Beloved — Time after Time
Beloved — You've Got Me Thinking
Duran Duran — Serious
Duran Duran — Violence of Summer
Enigma — Age of Loneliness (Carly's Song)
Everything but the Girl — Wrong
Happy Mondays — Step On
>> Lauryn Hill — Doo-Wop (That) Thing
Billy Idol — Speed
INXS — Strangest Party
New Order — State of the Union
Sinead O'Connor — Famine
Boz Scaggs — Some Change
Seal — Crazy
Seal — Future Love Paradise
Soul II Soul — Back to Life
Soul II Soul — Get a Life
Soul II Soul — I Can See
Soul II Soul — Jazzies Groove
Soul II Soul — Missing You
Spandau Ballet — Raw
Spice Girls — No.1 Low Band
Spice Girls — 2 Become 1
Spice Girls — Mamma
Lisa Stansfeld — This Is the Right Time
10,000 Maniacs — These Are the Days
Terence Trent D'Arby — Do You Love Me
>> The Wallflowers — Three Marlenas

JIM BLASHFIELD

Marc Cohn — Walk through the World
>> Peter Gabriel — Don't Give Up
Michael Jackson — Leave Me Alone
>> Joni Mitchell — Good Friends
Nu Shooz — I Can't Wait
Paul Simon — Boy in the Bubble
>> Talking Heads — And She Was
Tears for Fears — Sowing the Seeds of Love

GAVIN BOWDEN

Agents of Good Roots — Come On
Tatyana Ali — Daydreamin'
Blues Traveler — Canadian Rose
Buster Poindexter — Ondine
Butthole Surfers — Pepper
Dishwalla — Charlie Brown's Parents
Melanie Doane — Adam's Rib
Eve 6 — Leech
Fun Lovin' Criminals — Scooby Snacks
Chantal Kreviazuk — Wayne
Lit — My Own Worst Enemy

>> Live — Lakini's Juice
Low & Sweet Orchestra — Sometimes the Truth
Matchbox 20 — 3 A.M.
Orange 9mm — Failure
Orbit — Medicine
>> Rage Against the Machine — No Shelter
Red Hot Chili Peppers — Aeroplane
Red Hot Chili Peppers — Coffee Shop
Red Hot Chili Peppers — If You Have to Ask
Red Hot Chili Peppers — My Friends
Red Hot Chili Peppers — Suck My Kiss
>> Red Hot Chili Peppers — Warped
Rocket from the Crypt — On a Rope
Rollins Band — End of Something
Silverchair — Anthem for the Year 2000
Smash Mouth — Waste
Stroke 9 — Little Black Backpack
Tripping Daisy — Piranha

PAUL BOYD

Bryan Adams — The Best of Me
B-Tribe — You Won't See Me Cry
Blind Melon — I Wonder
Blind Melon — Dear Ole Dad
Brand New Heavies — You've Got a Friend
The Cult — Heart of Soul
The Cult — The Witch
The Cult — Coming Down
Des'ree — You Gotta Be
Digable Planets — Where I'm From
Divinyls — I'm on Your Side
Divinyls — Make Out Alright
Dubstar — Stars
Everclear — Heroin Girl
Josh Clayton Felt — Windows
Kyosuke Himuro — Ballad No. 2
Ice T — I Must Stand
INXS — Baby Don't Cry
INXS — Everything
Jamiroquai — Half the Man
Lenny Kravitz — Stand by My Woman
Mike and the Mechanics — Word of Mouth
Kylie Minogue — Confide in Me
911 — How Do You Want Me to Love You
The Rembrandts — Johnny
Right Said Fred — Hands Up for Lovers
The Roots — Clones
The Roots — Proceed
>> Seal — A Prayer for the Dying
Seiko — Good for You
Seiko — The Moment We Say Goodbye
Simply Red w/ the Fugees — Angel
Sting — Desert Rose
Tina Turner — When the Heartache Is Over
Shania Twain — From This Moment On
Shania Twain — Man, I Feel Like a Woman
Shania Twain — That Don't Impress Me
Shania Twain — You've Got a Way
Chris Whitley — Oh God My Heart Is Ready Now
Wild Colonials — Charm
Paul Young — Hope in a Hopeless World

PETER CARE

ABC — Be Near Me
ABC — Ocean Blue
ABC — Vanity Kills
Anita Baker — 24 Hours
Bananarama — More than Physical
Bananarama — Trick of the Night
Bananarama — Venus
Cabaret Voltaire — Big Funk
Cabaret Voltaire — Crackdown
Cabaret Voltaire — Don't Argue
Cabaret Voltaire — Hypnotized
Cabaret Voltaire — I Want You
Cabaret Voltaire — Just Fascination
Cabaret Voltaire — Kino
Cabaret Voltaire — Sensoria
Belinda Carlisle — Leave a Light On
Robert Cray — Smokin' Gun
Depeche Mode — Shake the Disease
Depeche Mode — Stripped
Thomas Dolby — May the Cube Be with You
Fine Young Cannibals — Funny How Love Is
Fine Young Cannibals — Good Thing
Fine Young Cannibals — I'm Not the Man
Fine Young Cannibals — In Concert (Live)
Los Lobos — One Time One Night
Richard Marx — Keep Coming Back
Eddie Money — Walk on Water
Robbie Neville — C'est la Vie
New Order — Regret
Roy Orbison — I Drove All Night
>> Tom Petty — It's Good to Be King
Public Image Limited — Rise
>> R.E.M. — Drive
R.E.M. — Electrolite (co-directed with Spike Jonze)
>> R.E.M. — Man on the Moon
R.E.M. — Radio Song
>> R.E.M. — What's the Frequency, Kenneth?
Scritti Politti — Hypnotized
Simply Red — Maybe Someday
Bruce Springsteen — Secret Garden
Tina Turner — I Don't Wanna Fight
Tina Turner — What You Get Is What You See
Tina Turner — Why Must We Wait until Tonight
Suzanne Vega — When Heroes Go Down

director.

video.

ANTON CORBIJN

Bryan Adams — Do I Have to Say the Words?
Bryan Adams — Have You Ever Really Loved a Woman?
Art of Noise — Beatbox
Grant Lee Buffalo — Mockingbirds
Naomi Campbell — Love & Tears
Johnny Cash — Delia's Gone
Nick Cave — Straight to You
Danzig — Dirty Black Summer
Depeche Mode — Barrel of a Gun
Depeche Mode — Behind the Wheel
Depeche Mode — Condemnation
Depeche Mode — Enjoy the Silence
Depeche Mode — Halo
Depeche Mode — I Feel You
Depeche Mode — In Your Room
Depeche Mode — It's No Good

director.

video.

Depeche Mode — Never Let Me Down Again
Depeche Mode — Personal Jesus
Depeche Mode — Policy of Truth
Depeche Mode — A Question of Time
Depeche Mode — Strangelove
Depeche Mode — Useless
Depeche Mode — Walking in My Shoes
Depeche Mode — World in My Eyes
Echo & The Bunnymen — The Game
Echo & The Bunnymen — Lips Like Sugar
Echo & The Bunnymen — Seven Seas
Front 242 — Headhunter
Front 242 — Tragedy for You
Herbert Gronemeyer — Marie
Garland Jeffreys — Hail Hail Rock 'n' Roll
Joy Division — Atmosphere
Ian McCulloch — Lover Lover Lover
Metallica — Hero of the Day
Metallica — Mama Said
Joni Mitchell and Peter Gabriel — My Secret Place
>> Nirvana — Heart Shaped Box
Red Hot Chili Peppers — My Friends
>> Rollins Band — Liar
Roxette — Stars
Roxette — Salvation
David Sylvian — Red Guitar
David Sylvian — The Ink in the Well
U2 — One
U2 — Please

director: **LOL CREME**

(see also Godley & Creme)

video: Joan Armatrading — The Weakness in Me
Joan Armatrading — When I Get It Right
Asia — In the Heat of the Moment
Asia — Only Time Will Tell
Go West — I Want to Hear It from You
Go West — We Close Our Eyes
Herbie Hancock — Autodrive
Elton John — Kiss the Bride
Tom Jones — If I Only Knew
Graham Parker — Temporary Beauty
Seal — Newborn Friend
Ringo Starr — The Cooler
Sting — I'm So Happy, I Can't Stop Crying
10cc — Feel the Love
Tina Turner — Simply the Best

director: **CHRIS CUNNINGHAM**

video: >> Aphex Twin — Come to Daddy
Autechre — Second Bad Vilbel
The Auteurs — Back with the Killer Again
The Auteurs — Light Aircraft on Fire
>> Björk — All Is Full of Love
Dubstar — No More Talk
Gene — Fighting Fit
Geneva — Tranquilizer
Holy Barbarians — Space Junkies
Jesus Jones — Next Big Thing
Jocasta — Something to Say
Leftfield — Africa (Shox)
Life's Addiction — Jesus Coming in for the Kill
Lodestar — Another Day

Madonna — Frozen
Placebo — 36 Degrees
>> Portishead — Only You
>> Squarepusher — Come on My Selector
12 Rounds — Personally

TAMRA DAVIS

Tatyana Ali w/ Will Smith — Boy You Knock Me Out
The Amps — Pacer
The Bangles — In Your Room
Beavis and Butthead w/ Cher — I've Got You, Babe
Boss Hog — I Dig You
Depeche Mode — But Not Tonight
DOC-NWA — It's Funky Enough
DOC-NWA w/ Dr. Dre — The Doc and the Doctor
Hanson — Mmmbop
Hanson — Where Is the Love
Hüsker Dü — Could You Be the One
Indigo Girls — Closer to Fine
Etta James — Beware
Ben Lee — Away with the Pixies
The Lemonheads — It's About Time
>> Luscious Jackson — City Song
>> Luscious Jackson — Ladyfingers
M.C. Lyte — Cha Cha Cha
Bette Midler — From a Distance
New Kids on the Block — Call It What You Want
Lou Reed — Busload of Faith
>> Veruca Salt — All Hail Me
The Smiths — Shoplifters Unite
>> Sonic Youth — 100% (w/ Spike Jonze)
Sonic Youth — Bull in the Heather
Sonic Youth — Dirty Boots and Kool Thing
Soul Asylum — Cartoon
Tone Loc — Funky Cold Medina
Tone Loc — Wild Thing
Young M.C. — Bust a Move

**JONATHAN DAYTON
& VALERIE FARIS**

Beastie Boys — Shadrach
Extreme — Hole Hearted
Extreme — More than Words
>> Neil Finn — She Will Have Her Way
Janet Jackson — Janet Documentary
Janet Jackson — Project 1814: Rhythm Nation
Lollapolooza — Documentary
>> Oasis — All Around the World
>> Porno for Pyros — Pets
Ramones — I Don't Want to Grow Up
Ramones — Spiderman Theme Song
R.E.M. — Star 69
R.E.M. — Tongue
R.E.M. — Tour Film
>> Smashing Pumpkins — 1979
Smashing Pumpkins — Rocket
Smashing Pumpkins — The End Is the
     Beginning Is the End
>> Smashing Pumpkins — Tonight, Tonight
Soundgarden — Outshined
Ringo Starr — Weight of the World
Sting — Sting Unplugged
Wayne's World — Ballroom Blitz

GERARD DE THAME

Black — Everything Is Coming Up Roses
>> Black — Wonderful Life
Sting — Mad About You
Sting — Soul Cages
Sting — Why Should I Cry
>> Tanita Tikaram — Cathedral Song
Tanita Tikaram — Twist in My Sobriety
Tia Maria — Images

NIGEL DICK

Ace of Base — Cruel Summer
Bryan Adams — I'm Ready
Backstreet Boys — All That I Have to Give
Cher — Strong Enough
Cher — Believe
Cool for August — Walk Away
Alice Cooper — Bed of Nails
Alice Cooper — Poison
The Corrs — Only When I Sleep
The Corrs — What Can I Do?
Cowboy Junkies — Angel Mine
D-Generation — No Way Out
Def Leppard — Rocket
Def Leppard — Work It Out
Celine Dion — It's All Coming Back to Me Now
Gloria Estefan — Feat
5ive — It's the Things You Do
5ive — When the Lights Go Out
Guns & Roses — Paradise City
Guns & Roses — Patience
Guns & Roses — Sweet Child o' Mine
Guns & Roses — Welcome to the Jungle
Hootie and the Blowfish — Only Lonely
Enrique Iglesias — Bailamos
Kula Shaker — Tattva
Mansun — Wide Open Spaces
Ricky Martin — She's All I Ever Had
>> Matchbox 20 — Push
N'Sync — Music of My Heart
Oasis — Champagne Supernova
>> Oasis — Don't Go Away
Oasis — Rock & Roll Superstar
>> Oasis — Wonderwall
The Offspring — Gone Away
Ozzy Osbourne — Back on Earth
R.E.M. — At My Most Beautiful
>> Savage Garden — I Want You
Savage Garden — To the Moon & Back (versions 1 & 2)
Social Distortion — When the Angels Sing
Britney Spears — Baby One More Time
Britney Spears — Crazy
Tears for Fears — Everybody Wants to Rule the World
Tears for Fears — Head Over Heels
Tears for Fears — Shout
>> Third Eye Blind — How's It Going To Be

Dom & Nic

The Bluetones — Bluetonic
>> David Bowie and Trent Reznor — I'm Afraid of
     Americans

The Chemical Brothers — Block Rockin' Beats
The Chemical Brothers — Setting Sun
The Chemical Brothers — Hey Boy Hey Girl
Lodger — Small Change
The Mystics — Lucy's Factory
The Mystics — See You
The Mystics — Who's That Girl
Oasis — D'You Know What I Mean
Smashing Pumpkins — Ava Adore
Supergrass — Late in the Day
Supergrass — Alright
Supergrass — Caught by the Fuzz
Supergrass — Going Out
Supergrass — Lenny
Supergrass — Mansize Rooster
Supergrass — Time
The Wallflowers — Heroes
Robbie Williams — She's the One

JESSE DYLAN

David Baerwald — All for You
The Black Crowes — Hotel Illness
Breathe — Does She Love That Man
» Nick Cave and the Bad Seeds — Red Right Hand
Bob Dylan — Most of the Time
Lita Ford — Hungry
Lenny Kravitz — It Ain't Over till It's Over
Lenny Kravitz — Mama Said
Maria Mckee — To Miss Someone
Michael Penn — This and That
Tom Petty — Face in the Crowd
Sam Phillips — Lying
P.I.L. — Don't Ask Me
P.M. Dawn — A Watcher's Point of View
Skid Row — Little Wing
Third Bass — Pop Goes the Weasel
» Tom Waits — Goin' Out West
The Wallflowers — Ashes to Ashes
Wendy & Lisa — Don't Try to Tell Me

NICK EGAN

Bananarama — Long Train Running
The Bee Gees — Alone
Better Than Ezra — Desperately Wanting
Bon Jovi — Dry Country
Bon Jovi — I Believe
Candlebox — Cover Me
Candlebox — Far Behind
Candlebox — It's Alright
Belinda Carlisle — Do You Feel Like I Feel
Belinda Carlisle — Little Black Book
Belinda Carlisle — Live Your Life, Be Free
Cheap Trick — You're All I Wanna Do
Terence Trent D'Arby — Vibrator
Deftones — Bored
Digable Planets — Nickel Bags
Duran Duran — Ordinary World
Duran Duran — Perfect Day
Duran Duran — White Lines
EMF — Children
EMF — Unbelievable
INXS — Don't Loose Your Head
INXS — Searching
Mick Jagger — Primitive Cool

» Manbreak — Ready or Not
Kylie Minogue — Step Back in Time
» Alanis Morissette — You Oughta Know
Motley Crue — Hooligan's Holiday
Ivan Neville — Not Just Another Girl
Oasis — Live Forever
Oasis — Supersonic
P.M. Dawn — Sometimes I Miss You So Much
Iggy Pop — Real Wild Child
» Rancid — Bloodclot
Duncan Sheik — Wishful Thinking
Silverchair — Abuse Me
Sonic Youth — Sugar Kane
Sonic Youth — Youth Against Fascism
Soup Dragons — Divine Thing
Soup Dragons — One Way Street
Soup Dragons — Pleasure
Tony, Toni, Tone — Anniversary
UB40 — Tell Me Is It True
Wendy & Lisa — Are You My Baby
Wendy & Lisa — Honeymoon Express
Wendy & Lisa — Lolly Lolly
Yazz and Aswad — How Long

David Fincher

Paula Abdul — Cold Hearted
Paula Abdul — Forever Your Girl
Paula Abdul — It's Just the Way That You Love Me
Paula Abdul — Straight Up
Aerosmith — Janie's Got a Gun
Bourgeois Tagg — I Don't Mind at All
Nenah Cherry — Heart
Martha Davis — Don't Tell Me the Time
Martha Davis — Tell It to the Moon
Foreigner — Say You Will
Colin Hay — Can I Hold You
Don Henley — The End of Innocence
The Hooters — Johnny B
» Billy Idol — Cradle of Love
Billy Idol — L.A. Women
Michael Jackson — Who Is It?
Johnny Hates Jazz — Heart of Gold
Johnny Hates Jazz — Shattered Dreams
Mark Knopfler and Willie De Ville — Princess Bride
Loverboy — Love Will Rise Again
Loverboy — Notorious
Madonna — Bad Girl
» Madonna — Express Yourself
Madonna — Oh, Father
» Madonna — Vogue
» George Michael — Freedom 90
Eddie Money — Endless Night
Roy Orbison — Mystery Girl
» Iggy Pop — Home
» The Rolling Stones — Love Is Strong
Patty Smyth — Downtown Train
Sting — Englishman in New York
The Wallflowers — Sixth Avenue Heartache
Jody Watley — Most of All
Jody Watley — Real Love
Steve Winwood — Holding On
Steve Winwood — Roll with It
Wire Train — Should She Cry
Wire Train — She Comes On

JONATHAN GLAZER

Blur — The Universal
Nick Cave — Into My Arms
» Jamiroquai — Virtual Insanity
Massive Attack — Karmacoma
» Radiohead — Karma Police
» Radiohead — Street Spirit
U.N.K.L.E. — Rabbit in Your Headlights

KEVIN GODLEY
(see also Godley & Creme)

A3 — Woke Up This Morning
Bryan Adams — All I Want Is You
Bryan Adams — Can't Stop This Thing We Started
Bryan Adams — Thought I'd Died & Gone to Heaven
The Beatles — Real Love
The Black Crowes — By Your Side
Blur — Girls and Boys
Bono and Gavin Friday — In the Name of the Father
Boyzone — When the Going Gets Tough
Boyzone — You Needed Me
Kate Bush and Larry Adler — The Man I Love
» The Charlatans — Forever
Eric Clapton — My Father's Eyes
Adam Clayton and Larry Mullen — Mission: Impossible
Phil Collins — Dance into the Light
Deep Forest — Deep Forest
Erasure — Blue Savannah
Fine Young Cannibals — Don't Look Back
» Forest for the Trees — Dream
Gavin Friday — You, Me & World War III
Jean Michel Jarre — Oxygen 8
Wyclef Jean, featuring Bono — New Day (version 2)
Garland Jeffreys — Sexuality
Paul McCartney — C'mon People
Graham Parker — Wake Up Next to You
Sting — Fields of Gold
Sting — Set Them Free
Thompson Twins — Dr. Dream
Tonic — Soldier's Daughter
U2 — Lemon (version 3)
U2 — Even Better Than the Real Thing (version 1)
U2 — Hold Me Thrill Me Kiss Me Kill Me (with Maurice Linnane)
U2 — Numb (version 1)
» U2 — The Sweetest Thing

GODLEY & CREME
(see also Lol Creme; Kevin Godley)

Bono and Frank Sinatra — I've Got You Under My Skin
Eric Clapton — Forever Man
Culture Club — Victims
Duran Duran — Girls on Film
Duran Duran — View to Kill
Frankie Goes to Hollywood — Power of Love
Frankie Goes to Hollywood — Two Tribes
Peter Gabriel — Biko
Peter Gabriel and Kate Bush — Don't Give Up
Godley & Creme — Cry
Godley & Creme — Englishman in New York

director.
video.
director.
video.
director.
video.

Godley & Creme — Golden Boy
Godley & Creme — Little Piece of Heaven
Godley & Creme — Save Me a Mountain
Godley & Creme — 10,000 Angels
Godley & Creme — Wedding Bells
Godley & Creme — Wide Boy
>> Herbie Hancock — Rock-It
George Harrison — When We Was Fab
Patti Labelle — Oh People
Huey Lewis and the News — Hip to Be Square
Police — Don't Stand So Close to Me
>> Police — Every Breath You Take
Police — Wrapped Around Your Finger
Lou Reed — No Money Down
Sting — Set Them Free
David Sylvian — Forbidden Colours
Wang Chung — Everybody Have Fun Tonight
Yes — Leave It

director: **MICHEL GONDRY**

video:
>> Beck — Deadweight
Björk — Army of Me
Björk — Bachelorette
>> Björk — Human Behavior
Björk — Isobel
Björk — Joga
The Black Crowes — High Head Blues
The Chemical Brothers — Let Forever Be
Sheryl Crow — Change Would Do You Good
Daft Punk — Around the World
>> The Foo Fighters — Everlong
I Am — Je Danse le Mia
Wyclef Jean — Another One Bites the Dust
Lucas — Lucas with the Lid Off
Massive Attack — Protection
>> Cibo Matto — Sugar Water
Oasis — Stand by Me
Oui Oui — Les Cailloux
The Rolling Stones — Gimme Shelter
>> The Rolling Stones — Like a Rolling Stone
Stardust — The Music Sounds Better with You

director: **HOWARD GREENHALGH**

video:
>> Counting Crows — Daylight Fading
DCC — Sperm
Deep Forest — Marta's Song
Enigma — Rivers of Belief
Feline — Just As You Are
Gabrielle — Forget About the World
Genesis — Congo
INXS — Not Enough Time
Lush — Deluxe
Meat Loaf — I'd Lie for You
Meat Loaf — Not a Dry Eye
George Michael — Jesus to a Child
Mike Oldfield — Let There Be Light
OMD — Universal
OMD — Walking on the Milky Way
Pet Shop Boys — Before
Pet Shop Boys — Paninako
Pet Shop Boys — Single Bilingual
Pet Shop Boys — Yesterday When I Was
>> Placebo — Bruise Pristine

Placebo — Nancy Boy
Sneaker Pimps — Post Modern Sleaze
>> Soundgarden — Black Hole Sun
Sting — If I Ever Lose My Faith in You
Sting — When We Dance
Suede — Wild Ones
Suzanne Vega — In Liverpool

PAULA GREIF
(see also Greif & Kagan)

Paula Cole — Me
Shawn Colvin — I Don't Know Why
Julia Fordham — Comfort of Strangers
Julia Fordham — Happy Ever After
Julia Fordham — Love Moves in Mysterious Ways
Julia Fordham — Where Does the Time Go
Lalah Hathaway — Baby Don't Cry
John Hiatt — Buffalo River Home
The Jesus & Mary Chain — Her Way of Praying
Billy Joel — I Go to Extremes
Lenny Kravitz — Rock the Vote
London Beat — Better Love
London Beat — I've Been Thinking About You
Madonna — Rock the Vote
Ziggy Marley — Look Who's Dancing
Ziggy Marley — Tomorrow People
Merchants of Venice — Say Ah
The Neville Brothers — One More Day
New Order — Round & Round
Teddy Pendergrass — Glad to Be Alive
>> Iggy Pop — Wild America
Keith Richards — Make No Mistake
Carly Simon — Love of My Life
Soul II Soul — Keep on Moving
Keith Sweat — Make You Sweat
Suzanne Vega — Men in a War
The Wallflowers — Be Your Own Girl
Chris Whitley — Poison Girl
Paul Young — Heaven Can Wait

GREIF & KAGAN
(see also Paula Greif; Peter Kagan)

DEE-Lite — Rock the Vote
The Dream Academy — Love Parade
The Dream Academy — This World
>> Duran Duran — Skin Trade
Cutting Crew — (I Just) Died in Your Arms Tonight
Steve Winwood — Higher Love

MICHAEL HAUSSMAN

Paula Abdul — My Love Is for Real
Joe Cocker — When Night Calls
Chris Isaak — Can't Do Anything
>> Madonna — Take a Bow
Madonna — You'll See
Martika — Love Thy Will Be Done
Michael McDonald — Tear It Up
New Legend — Angel of Mercy
Sidewinders — Witchdoctor
Wet Wet Wet — Stay with Me Heartache

DAVID HOGAN

Blues Traveler — Conquer Me
Bob Seger — Like a Rock
Cake — Big Strange
Charles & Eddie — A House
The Church — Under the Milky Way
Mark Cohn — Already Home
Shawn Colvin — Every Little Thing
Sheryl Crow — All I Wanna Do
>> Sheryl Crow — Leaving Las Vegas
Melissa Etheridge — Your Little Secret
Melissa Etheridge — You're the Only One
John Fogerty — Walking in a Hurricane
Gin Blossoms — Day Job
Gin Blossoms — Found Out About You
Goo Goo Dolls — Long Way Down
Goo Goo Dolls — Naked
Tom Jones — I Wanna Get Back
Aimee Mann — That's Just What You Are
Dave Matthews Band — Ants Marching
Dave Matthews Band — What Would You Say?
Steve Miller Band — From the 20s
>> Steve Miller Band — Ya Ya
Aaron Neville — Don't Fall
Lionel Richie — Time
Diana Ross — Your Love
Joe Satriani — All Alone
Rod Stewart — So Far Away
Supertramp — You Win, I Lose
The Tuesdays — It's Up to You
>> Shania Twain — You're Still the One

PAUL HUNTER

Aaliya — Got to Give It Up
Aaliya — One in a Million
Babyface — You Were There
>> Erykah Badu — On and On
Blackstreet — Fix
Mary J. Blige — Love Is All We Need
Boyz II Men — Four Seasons of Loneliness
Boyz II Men — I Can't Let Her Go
Mariah Carey — Honey
D'Angelo — Untitled
Celine Dion — I Want You to Need Me
Jermaine Dupri — The Party Continues
Missy Elliot — Hit 'em wit da Hee
Faith Evans — All Night Long
Everclear — Father of Mine
Flipmode Squad — Cha, Cha, Cha
Warren G. — I Shot the Sheriff
Warren G. — Smoking Me Out
Warren G. — I Want It All
Johnny Gill — It's Your Body
Heavy D — Big Daddy
Lauryn Hill — Sweet Things
Hole — Malibu
Whitney Houston — Step by Step
Ice Cube — We Be Clubbin'
Enrique Iglesias — Bailamos
Janet Jackson — I Get Lonely
Lenny Kravitz — American Woman
>> Lenny Kravitz — Fly Away
LL Cool J — Hot, Hot, Hot

>> LL Cool J — Phenomenon
Jennifer Lopez — Feelin' So Good
Jennifer Lopez — If You Had My Love
Marilyn Manson — I Don't Like the Drugs but the
    Drugs Like Me
>> Marilyn Manson — The Dope Show
Matchbox 20 — Back 2 Good
Notorious B.I.G. — Hypnotize
Puff Daddy — Best Friend
Puff Daddy — Can't Nobody Hold Me Down
Puff Daddy — It's All About the Benjamins
Puff Daddy and the Family — Been Around the World
Busta Rhymes — Turn It Up/Fire It Up
Salt 'n' Pepa — Gitty Up
Will Smith — Wild, Wild West
Keith Sweat — I'm Not Ready
Keith Sweat — Just a Touch
Tamia — Imagination
Tamia — Make Tonight a Beautiful Night
TLC — Unpretty
Tribe Called Quest — Find My Way

PHIL JOANOU

Bon Jovi — Keep the Faith
Whitney Houston and Mariah Carey — When You
    Believe
>> Tom Petty — Walls (Circus Mix)
Tom Petty — You Don't Know How It Feels
U2 — If God Will Send His Angels
U2 — Merry Christmas (Baby Please Come Home)
>> U2 — One
>> U2 — Wild Horses
U2 and B.B. King — When Love Comes to Town

SPIKE JONZE

>> Beastie Boys — Sabotage
Beastie Boys — Sure Shot
Beastie Boys — Time for Living
>> Björk — It's Oh So Quiet
Blind Skateboards — Video Days
The Breeders — Cannonball
The Breeders — Divine Hammer
Chainsaw Kittens — High in High School
The Chemical Brothers — Electrobank
Chocolate Skateboards — Las nueve vidas de paco
Daft Punk — Da Funk
Dinosaur Jr. — Feel the Pain
Fatboy Slim — You've Come a Long Way, Baby
Elastica — Car Song
Girls Skateboards — Goldfish
Hurricane — Stick 'em Up
M.C. 900 Foot Jesus — If I Only Had a Brain
>> Notorious B.I.G. — Sky's the Limit
Pavement — Shady Lane
Pharcyde — Drop
R.E.M. — Crush with Eyeliner
R.E.M. — Electrolite (co-directed with Peter Care)
Sonic Youth — 100% (w/ Tamra Davis)
Teenage Fan Club — Hang On
Velocity Girl — I Can't Stop Smiling
Mike Watt — Big Train
Mike Watt — Liberty Calls
>> Wax — California

Wax — Hush
Ween — Freedom of '76
Weezer — Buddy Holly
Weezer — Undone: The Sweater Song
X — Country at War

PETER KAGAN
(see also Greif & Kagan)

Aftershock — Always Thinkin' About You
Marshall Crenshaw — Little Wild One
Christopher Cross — That Girl
The Del Fuegos — I Still Want You
Duran Duran — Notorious
Duran Duran — El Presedente
The Graces — Lay Down Your Arms
Julian Lennon — This is My Day
Heather Nova — London Rain
Sam Phillips — Holding on to the Earth
Scritti Pollitti — Perfect Way
Rosie Vela — Magic Smile
Rosie Vela — Interlude

DEAN KARR

Danzig — I Don't Mind the Pain
The Deftones — My Own Summer
Duran Duran — Out of My Mind
Filter — Jurassitol
John Forte — Ninety-Nine
Godsmack — Voodoo
Hide — Electric Cucumber
Sass Jordan — Pissin' Down
John Lennon and Cheap Trick — I'm Losing You
Love & Rockets — Sweet Love Hangover
>> Marilyn Manson — Sweet Dreams (Are Made of This)
>> Dave Matthews Band — Crash into Me
Dave Matthews Band — Crush
>> Dave Matthews Band — Don't Drink the Water
Dave Matthews Band — Stay
Ozzy Osbourne — I Just Want You
Ozzy Osbourne and Coal Chamber — Shock the
    Monkey
Screaming Trees — Sworn and Broken
Soul Assassins — Puppetmaster
Tea Party — Fire in the Head
The Verve Pipe — Villains

KEVIN KERSLAKE

Bush — Glycerine
Depeche Mode — One Caress
Dinosaur Jr. — Goin' Home
Everclear — Everything to Everyone
Faith No More — Midlife Crisis
Filter — Hey Man Nice Shot
Green Day — Brain Stew
Green Day — Jaded
Sophie B. Hawkins — California Here I Come
Helmet — Unsung
Hole — Garbage Man
Insane Clown Posse — Halls of Illusions
k.d. lang — If I Were You
Magnificent Bastards — Mockingbird Girl

>> Mazzy Star — Fade into You
Mazzy Star — Flowers in December
Mazzy Star — Halah
Mr. Bungle — Travolta
>> Nirvana — Come As You Are
>> Nirvana — In Bloom
The Offspring — The Meaning of Life
Pantera — This Love
>> Sam Phillips — I Need Love
Iggy Pop — High on You
>> Red Hot Chili Peppers — Soul to Squeeze
>> R.E.M. — Sidewinder Sleeps Tonite
The Rolling Stones — I Go Wild
Simple Minds — She's a River
Smashing Pumpkins — Cherub Rock
Sonic Youth — Beauty Lies in the Eyes
Sonic Youth — Candle
Sonic Youth — Shadow of a Doubt
Soul Asylum — Sometime to Return
Soundgarden — Hands All Over
Soundgarden — Loud Love
>> Stone Temple Pilots — Interstate Love Song
>> Stone Temple Pilots — Vasoline
Throwing Muses — Bright Yellow Gun
Urban Dance Squad — Deeper Shade of Soul

MARY LAMBERT

The Devlins — Heavens Wall
Eurythmics — Would I Lie to You?
Elysian Fields — Jack in the Box
The Go-Go's — Turn to You
The Go-Go's — Yes or No
Debbie Harry — I Want That Man
Chris Isaak — Dancin'
Janet Jackson — Control
Janet Jackson — Nasty Boys
Mick Jagger — Say You Will
Mick Jagger — Throwaway
Laila — Here We Go Again
Live — Turn My Head
Madonna — Borderline
Madonna — La Isla Bonita
>> Madonna — Like a Prayer
Madonna — Like a Virgin
Madonna — Material Girl
Motley Crue — Don't Go Away Mad
Motley Crue — Without You
Robbie Robertson — What About Now
Sting — We'll Be Together Tonight

FRANCIS LAWRENCE

Aerosmith — I Don't Want to Miss a Thing
Bad Religion — 10 in 2010
The Braxtons — Only Love
Tevin Campbell — I Got It Bad
Natalie Cole — A Smile Like Yours
Color Me Badd — Sexual Capacity
Coolio — When You Get There
En Vogue — Too Gone, Too Long
Fastball — Fire Escape
Foreigner — All I Need to Know
>> Ginuwine — What's So Different
Lauryn Hill — Turn Your Lights Down Low

director.

video.

director.

video.

0 : 0 2 : 6 1

Enrique Iglesias — Rhythm Divine
Jay-Z — Girl's Best Friend
Wyclef Jean — Gone 'til November
Jennifer Lopez — Waiting for Tonight
Ricky Martin — Private Emotion
» Maxwell — Fortunate
Brian McKnight — Back at One
Sarah McLachlan — Adia
Melanie C. — Never Be the Same Again
Monica — For You I Will
112 w/ Mase — Love M
Organized Noise — Set It Off
Pras — Ghetto Supastar
Robyn — Do You Really Want Me?
» Seal — Human Beings
Third Eye Blind — Losing a Whole Year
Timbaland w/ Missy & Magoo — Here We Come
Vanessa Williams — Happiness

director.
video.

LESLIE LIBMAN & LARRY WILLIAMS

The Bangles — Manic Monday
The Bangles — Ordinary Lives
» The Bee Gees — You Win Again
Edie Brickell — Circle
Jackson Browne — For America
T-Bone Burnett — The Murder Mystery
» Belinda Carlisle — Mad About You
Kim Carnes — You Make My Heart Beat Faster
The Church — Columbus
The Church — Tantalized
The Cult — Lil' Devil
Chicago — You're the Inspiration
Chick Corea and Gary Burton — Finale
David & David — Swallowed by the Cracks
David & David — Welcome to the Boomtown
The Dream Academy — Life in a Northern Town
The Dream Academy — Please, Please, Please
Michael Franks — Your Secret's Safe with Me
Boy George — Keep Me in Mind
Al Green — As Long As We're Together
Al Green — Everything's Gonna Be Alright
Sammy Hagar — Two Sides of Love
Heaven 17 — Contenders
Heaven 17 — Trouble
Jimi Hendrix — Voo Doo Child
Al Jarreau — After All
Kitaro — Cloud
k.d. lang — Pullin' Back the Reins
Ziggy Marley — Lee & Molly
Ziggy Marley — Tumblin' Down
Michael McDonald — Every Beat of My Heart
Michael McDonald — Lost in the Parade
The Models — Evolution
Ennio Morricone — The Mission
Ennio Morricone — Williowns Theme
OMD — Forever Live and Die
OMD — Shame
Roy Orbison — Crying
Roy Orbison — In Dreams
Roy Orbison — You Got It
» Iggy Pop — Living on the Edge of the Night
Prince — When Doves Cry
Keith Richards — Take It So Hard
Little Richard — Operator
David Sanborn — Love and Happiness

Brenda Russell — Gravity
Paul Simon — Homeless
Paul Simon — You Can Call Me Al
Rod Stewart — Another Heartache
Rod Stewart — Every Beat of My Heart
Joe Strummer — Walker
Suzanne Vega — Marlene in the Wall

MATT MAHURIN

Alice in Chains — Angry Chair
Alice in Chains — No Excuses
David Baerwald — All for You
Blind Melon — Dear Ol' Dad
Bush — Everything Zen
» Bush — Little Things
Tracy Chapman — Fast Car
Cowboy Junkies — Sweet Jane (version 1)
Def Leppard — All I Want Is Everything
Peter Gabriel — Come Talk to Me
Peter Gabriel — Mercy Street
Peter Gabriel — Red Rain
» Hole — Gold Dust Woman
INXS and Ray Charles — Please (You Got That . . .)
    (version 2)
Metallica — King Nothing
Metallica — The Unforgiven II
Motley Crue — Home Sweet Home (version 2: 1991
    Remix)
The Nixons — Happy Song
The Nixons — Sister
Queensryche — Another Rainy Night (version 2)
Queensryche — Best I Can
Queensryche — Bridge
Queensryche — Empire
Queensryche — Silent Lucidity
Bonnie Raitt — Love Will Lead the Way
Bonnie Raitt — One Belief Away
Bonnie Raitt — Something to Talk About
Bonnie Raitt and Bruce Hornsby — I Can't Make You
    Love Me
Lou Reed — Hookywooky
Lou Reed — What's Good? (The Thesis)
R.E.M. — Orange Crush
Soul Asylum — Misery
Soundgarden — The Day I Tried to Live
Therapy? — Die Laughing
Urge Overkill — Take a Walk
U2 — Love Is Blindness
U2 — With or Without You (version 2: B&W)
Tom Waits — Hold On

JOHN MAYBURY

Marc Almond — Desperate Hours
Marc Almond — Waifs and Strays
Neneh Cherry — Buffalo Stance
Neneh Cherry — Kisses in the Wind
Neneh Cherry — Money Love
The Cranberries — Dreams
Erasure — Star
Everything but the Girl — Each & Everyone
Everything but the Girl — Mine
Everything but the Girl — Those Early Days
Boy George — No Clause 28

Boy George — Everything I Own (new video for re-release)
Boy George — Il Adore
Boy George — Living My Life
The Jesus & Mary Chain — Happy When It Rains
The Jesus & Mary Chain — Sidewalking
Jesus Jones — Bring It on Down
Cindy Lauper — World Is Stone
Morrissey — Our Frank
Shara Nelson — Down That Road
» Shara Nelson — One Goodbye in Ten
Sinead O'Connor — Mandinka
Sinead O'Connor — Emperor's New Clothes
Sinead O'Connor — I Want Your Hands on Me
Sinead O'Connor — Jump in the River
Sinead O'Connor — My Special Child
» Sinead O'Connor — Nothing Compares to U
Sinead O'Connor — This is to Mother You
Sinead O'Connor — Three Babies
Sinead O'Connor — Troy
Sinead O'Connor — You Do Something to Me
Rifat Ozbeck Electronic Fashion Show — Affrodizia
Rifat Ozbeck Electronic Fashion Show — Millennium
Ryuichi Sakamoto — Love Is the Devil
The Smiths — There Is a Light That Never Goes Out
Thompson Twins — Come Inside

Melodie McDaniel

Tori Amos — God
The Cranberries — Linger
Lisa Germano — Puppet
Jazz Lee — Love . . . Never That
Annie Lennox — Mama
» Madonna — Secret
Mazzy Star — She's My Baby
M.C. 900 Foot Jesus — But If You Go
Natalie Merchant — Carnival
» Porno for Pyros — Cursed Female
» Patti Smith — Don't Smoke in Bed
Catherine Wheel — Show Me Mary

KEIR MCFARLANE

The Bell Jar — Love Like Rain
Boom Crash Opera — The Best Thing
C & C Music Factory — Do You Want to Get Funky
» Candlebox — Simple Lessons
Sheryl Crow — If It Makes You Happy
Crowded House — Better Be Home Soon
Falling Joys — Lock It and You're in a Mess
Gang Ga Jang — American Money
Gang Ga Jang — Luck of the Irish
Janet Jackson — Anytime, Anyplace
Janet Jackson — Twenty Foreplay
Janet Jackson — You Want This
John Kennedy — World Upside Down
Kylie Minogue — Put Yourself into My Place
» Tom Petty and the Heartbreakers — Mary Jane's
    Last Dance
The Radiators — Dreaming
The Radiators — Love Ain't Love
Spy vs. Spy — Clear Skies
UB40 — Bring Me Your Cup
The Wallflowers — One Headlight
Warren Zevon — Straight Down

JEAN-BAPTISTE MONDINO

Amina — Atame
Alain Bashung — Ma Petite Entreprise
Alain Bashung — Volutes
Alain Bashung — Osez Joséphine
Björk — Violently Happy
David Bowie — Never Let Me Down
Neneh Cherry — Manchild
Neneh Cherry — Buddy X
Neneh Cherry — I've Got You Under My Skin
Neneh Cherry — Kootchi
Alain Chamfort — L'ennemi dans la Glace
China — Time
Mark Curry — Sorry About the Weather
Bryan Ferry — Slave to Love
Jean-Paul Gaultier — How to Do That
Boy George — To Be Reborn
» Don Henley — Boys of Summer
Chris Isaak — You Owe Me Some Kind of Love
Jay — Born on the Wrong Side of Town
Jill Jones — Mia Bocca
Keziah Jones — Rhythm Is Love
Nick Kamen — Each Time You Break My Heart
Lenny Kravitz — Be
Lavoine and Ringer — Qu'est-ce que t'es Belle
» Madonna — Human Nature
» Madonna — Justify My Love
Madonna — Love Don't Live Here Anymore
Madonna — Open Your Heart
M.C. Solaar — Sequelles
» Me'shell Ndegéocello — If That's Your Boyfriend
    (He Wasn't Last Night)
Rita Mitsouko — Les Amants
Rita Mitsouko — C'est Comme Ça
Jean-Baptiste Mondino — La Danse des Mots
Vanessa Paradis — Tandem
Vanessa Paradis — Natural High
Prince — I Wish U Heaven
Scritti Politti — Woodbeez
Sting — Russians
Telephone — Un Autre Monde
Tom Waits — Downtown Train
Zazie — Tout le Monde

SOPHIE MULLER

» Björk — Venus As a Boy
Blur — Beetlebum
Blur — Song II
Blur — On Your Own
Jeff Buckley — So Real
The Cure — The 13th
Curve — Coast Is Clear
Curve — Fait Accompli
Eurythmics — Angel
Eurythmics — Chill
Eurythmics — Don't Ask Me Why
Eurythmics — I Need a Man
Eurythmics — King and Queen of America
Eurythmics — Listen to Beethoven
Eurythmics — Wide Eyed Girl
Julia Fordham — Lock and Key
Nanci Griffith — Late Night Grand Hotel
Hole — Miss World
The Jesus & Mary Chain — Sometimes Always

Annie Lennox — Love Song for a Vampire
Annie Lennox — Little Bird
Annie Lennox — Precious
Annie Lennox — Walking on Broken Glass
» Annie Lennox — Why
Annie Lennox and Al Green — Put a Little Love
Lisa Loeb and Nine Stories — Do You Sleep
Maxwell — Whenever, Wherever, Whatever
Aaron Neville — Somewhere Somebody
No Doubt — Don't Speak
No Doubt — Excuse Me Mister
No Doubt — Live at the Tragic Kingdom
No Doubt — Sunday Morning
Sinead O'Connor — Emperor's New Clothes
Sade — No Ordinary Love
Sade — Love Is Stronger Than Pride
Sade — Turn My Back on You
Shakespeare's Sister — Break My Heart
Shakespeare's Sister — Goodbye Cruel World
Shakespeare's Sister — Hello
Shakespeare's Sister — I Can Drive
Shakespeare's Sister — I Didn't Care
Shakespeare's Sister — Run Silent Run Deep
Shakespeare's Sister — Stay
Dave Stewart — Out of Reach
Weezer — Say It Ain't So
World Party — Thank You World

DOUG NICHOL

» Aerosmith — Pink
The Cars — Strap Me In
Toni Childs — Many Rivers to Cross
Johnny Clegg and Savuka — Take My Heart Away
Etienne Daho — Des Attractions Desastres
Etienne Daho — Un Homme à la Mer
Etienne Daho — Ideal
Etienne Daho — Interlude à la Desirade
Etienne Daho — Le Premier Jour
Etienne Daho — Rue des Petits Hôtels
Etienne Daho — Zero et l'Infini
Chris de Burgh — Separate Tables
Del Amitri — Be My Downfall
Del Amitri — Kiss This Thing Goodbye
Des'ree — I Ain't Moving
Dutronc & Daho — Tous les Gouts Sont dans ma
    Nature
Extreme — Stop the World
Geri Halliwell — Mi Chico Latino
Patricia Kaas — Kennedy Rose
Kula Shaker — Mystical Machine Gun
Patti La Belle — Stir It Up
Shara Nelson — Rough with the Smooth
New Kids on the Block — Hangin' Tough
New Kids on the Block — I'll Be Loving You Forever
New Kids on the Block — Please Don't Go Girl
New Kids on the Block — The Right Stuff
Ray Parker Jr. — Girls Are More Fun
» Pulp — This Is Hardcore
Sting — Seven Days
Sting — Shape of My Heart
Tuck and Patti — Dreams
Tuck and Patti — Time After Time
Wet Wet Wet — More Than Love

MARCUS NISPEL director.

ABC — Say It video.
Ashford & Simpson — I'll Be There for You
Tony Bennett — Steppin' Out with My Baby
B-52s — Good Stuff
» Bush — Greedy Fly
Tevin Campbell — Always in My Heart
Mariah Carey — Make It Happen
Tia Carrere — I Never Even Told You
C & C Music Factory — Gonna Make You Sweat
    (Everybody Dance Now)
C & C Music Factory — Things That Make You Go
    Hmmm
Cher — One by One
Cher — Walking in Memphis
Chic — Your Love
Natalie Cole — Take a Look
Terence Trent D'Arby — Let Her Down Easy
Divinyls — Love School
En Vogue — Give It Up
Gloria Estefan — Turn the Beat Around
Faith No More — A Small Victory
Mylene Farmer — Come J'aimal
Aretha Franklin — Everybody
» The Fugees — Ready or Not
Gene Loves Jezebel — Josephina
Gipsy Kings — Escucha Me
Go West — Tracks of My Tears
Amy Grant and Vince Gill — House of Love
Nina Hagen — So Bad
Janet Jackson — Runaway
Billy Joel — Lullaby
Elton John — Believe
Brian Knight — Still in Love with You
k.d. lang — Sexuality
Lil' Kim — No Time
Lisa Lisa & Cult Jam — Let the Beat Hit 'Em
George Michael — Killer/Papa Was a Rolling Stone
Luis Miguel — Dame
» No Doubt — Spiderwebs
OMD — Stand Above Me
P.M. Dawn — You Got Me Floatin'
Puff Daddy — Victory
Right Said Fred — Bumped
Scorpions — You and I
Lisa Stansfield — Someday
Al B. Sure — Had Enough
Take 6 — You Are the Biggest Part of Me
Luther Vandross — Every Year, Every Christmas
Wet Wet Wet — Julia Says
Wet Wet Wet — Love Is All Around

MARK PELLINGTON director.

Alice in Chains — Rooster video.
Anthrax — Black Lodge
Leonard Cohen — Dance Me to the End of Love
The Connells — 74, 75
De La Soul — Say No Go
Disposable Heroes of Hiphoprisy — Television, Drug
    of Nation
Pete Droge — Beautiful Girl
Maggy Estep — Hey Baby
Agnes Gooch — Baby in Green
INXS — Beautiful Girl

Jungle Brothers — I Get a Kick Out of You
Lush — Lady Killer
>> Nine Inch Nails — We're in This Together
>> Pearl Jam — Jeremy
P.M. Dawn — Reality Used to Be a Friend
P.M. Dawn — Set Adrift on Memory Bliss
Public Enemy — Shut 'em Down
Screamin' Trees — Butterfly
Spearhead — Positive
>> U2 — One (buffalo version)
Whale — Hobo Humpin' Slobo Babe
Whale — Kickin'
Catherine Wheel — Way Down

director.

JEFFREY PLANSKER

video.

>> Belly — Slow Dog
The Grays — Very Best Years
The Jayhawks — Blue
Radiohead — Stop Whispering
>> Robbie Robertson — Mahk Jchi
>> Soundgarden — Spoonman
>> 10,000 Maniacs — Candy Everybody Wants
Jennifer Trynin — One Year Down
>> Urge Overkill — Positive Bleeding

director.

TIM POPE

video.

Marc Almond — Bittersweet
The Bangles — Eternal Flame
Bow Wow Wow — Do Ya Wanna Hold Me
David Bowie — Time Will Crawl
David Bowie/Adrian Belew — Pretty Pink Rose
Bronski Beat — C'mon C'mon
The Cars — Magic
The Cure — Boys Don't Cry
The Cure — Catch
The Cure — Caterpillar
The Cure — Close to Me
The Cure — Close to Me II
The Cure — Friday I'm in Love
The Cure — High
The Cure — Hot Hot Hot 12"
The Cure — In Between Days
The Cure — Just Like Heaven
The Cure — Let's Go to Bed
The Cure — Lone Song
>> The Cure — Lovecats
The Cure — Never Enough
The Cure — A Night Like This
The Cure — Pictures of You
The Cure — Staring at the Sea
The Cure — The Walk
The Cure — Why Can't I Be You
Dream Academy — Life in a Northern Town
Everything but the Girl — When All's Well
Bryan Ferry — Help Me
Bryan Ferry — Legend
Hall & Oates — Adult Education
Julian Lennon — Say You're Wrong
Live — I Alone
Paul McCartney — This One
Men Without Hats — Moon Beam
Men Without Hats — Pop Goes the World
Men Without Hats — Safety Dance

Men Without Hats — Where Do the Boys Go
Ministry — Revenge
The Nymphs — Sad & Damned
Iggy Pop — Kiss My Blood
Pop's Cool Love — Free Me
The Pretenders — 2,000 Miles
Psychedelic Furs — Angels Don't Cry
Psychedelic Furs — The Ghost in You
Psychedelic Furs — Heaven
Psychedelic Furs — Here Come the Cowboys
Psychedelic Furs — Love My Way
Queen — It's a Hard Life
Rush — After Image
Siouxie and the Banshees — Dazzle
Siouxie and the Banshees — Dear Prudence
Siouxie and the Banshees — Swimming Horses
Soft Cell — Bedsitter
Soft Cell — Down in the Subway
Soft Cell — Entertain Me
Soft Cell — Frustration
Soft Cell — Memorabilia
Soft Cell — Say Hello, Say Goodbye
Soft Cell — Secret Life
Soft Cell — Sex Dwarf
Soft Cell — Soul Inside
Soft Cell — Speedy Films
Soft Cell — Tainted Love
Soft Cell — Torch
Soft Cell — What
Soft Cell — Where Be the Heart
Spear of Destiny — The Wheel
The Strangers — 96 Tears
Style Council — Doot Doot
Style Council — Long Hot Summer
Style Council — Money Goround
Style Council — My Ever Changing Moods
Style Council — Shout to the Top
Style Council — Solid Bond
Style Council — Speak Like a Child
Style Council — Walls Come Tumbling Down
Style Council — You're the Best Thing
Talk Talk — Believe in You
Talk Talk — Dum Dum Girl
Talk Talk — Life's What You Make of It
Talk Talk — Living in Another World
Talk Talk — Such a Shame
The The — Gravitate Me
The The — Kingdom of Rain
The The — Slow Emotion Replay
The The — Slow Train to Dawn
The The — Twilight of a Champion
The The — Walk into the World
Tin Machine — Baby Universal
Tin Machine — You Belong in Rock 'n' Roll
Tom Tom Club — Suboceana
Bonnie Tyler — Loving You Is a Dirty Job
Wendy & Lisa — Sideshow
Wendy & Lisa — Waterfall
Wham — Young Guns (Go for It)
Neil Young — Cry, Cry, Cry
Neil Young — People on the Streets
Neil Young — Pressure
Neil Young — This Town
Neil Young — Touch the Night
Neil Young — Wanderin'
Neil Young — Weight of the World

ALEX PROYAS

Crowded House — Better Be Home Soon
Crowded House — Don't Dream It's Over
Cutting Crew — Everything but My Pride
Cutting Crew — Scattering
Fleetwood Mac — Everywhere
Colin Hay — Into My Life
>> INXS — Kiss the Dirt
Joe Jackson — 19 Forever
Medicine — Time Baby
Ivan Neville — Falling Out of Love
Mike Oldfield — Magic Touch
OMD — Dreaming
>> Sting — All This Time
Steve Winwood — I Will Be Here
Yes — Rhythm of Love

HERB RITTS

Jon Bon Jovi — Please Come Home for Christmas
Toni Braxton — Let It Flow
Mariah Carey — My All
Chris Isaak — Baby Did a Bad Thing
>> Chris Isaak — Wicked Game
>> Janet Jackson — Love Will Never Do Without You
Michael Jackson — Out of the Closet
>> Madonna — Cherish

MATTHEW ROLSTON

Bryan Adams — Chelsea Girls
Bryan Adams — The Only Thing That Looks Good on
    Me Is You
David Bowie — Miracle Goodnight
David Bowie — Nobody's Dancing
Brand New Heavies — Brother Sister
Sheryl Crow — There Goes the Neighborhood
En Vogue — Don't Let Go
En Vogue — My Loving
En Vogue — Whatever
The Foo Fighters — Walking After You
>> Garbage — I Think I'm Paranoid
Natalie Imbruglia — Wishing I Was There
Janet Jackson — Everytime
>> Jewel — Foolish Games
>> Lenny Kravitz — Thinking of You
Madonna — The Power of Goodbye
>> Marilyn Manson — Long Hard Road Out of Hell
Matchbox 20 — Real World
Morrissey — Alma Matters
Seal — Kiss From a Rose
TLC — Creep
TLC — Red Light Special

MARK ROMANEK

ABC — Love Conquers All
>> Fiona Apple — Criminal
>> Beck — Devil's Haircut
David Bowie — Black Tie, White Noise
David Bowie — Jump, They Say
De la Soul — Ring Ring Ring Ha Ha Hey

Definition of Sound — Moira Jane's Cafe
Eels — Novocaine for the Soul
En Vogue — Don't Worry About a Thing
En Vogue — Free Your Mind
G-Love & Special Sauce — Cold Beverage
Macy Gray — Do Something
Macy Gray — I Try (version 2)
Robyn Hitchcock — Madonna of the Wasps
Robyn Hitchcock — One Long Pair of Eyes
Janet Jackson — Got 'til It's Gone
Michael and Janet Jackson — Scream
Lenny Kravitz — Are You Gonna Go My Way?
>> Lenny Kravitz — If You Can't Say No
Lenny Kravitz — Is There Any Love in Your Heart
k.d. lang — Constant Craving
>> Madonna — Bedtime Story
Madonna — Rain
Michael McDonald — Take It to the Heart
>> Nine Inch Nails — Closer
>> Nine Inch Nails — Perfect Drug
Iggy Pop — Beside You
Pop's Cool Love — Buzz
R.E.M. — Strange Currencies
Keith Richards — Wicked as It Seems
Sonic Youth — Little Trouble Girl
Teenage Fanclub — What You Do to Me
The The — Sweet Bird of Truth
Weezer — El Scorcho
Steve Wynn — Carolyn

ROCKY SCHENCK

Ace of Base — Lucky Love
Afghan Whigs — Gentlemen
Alice in Chains — Grind
Alice in Chains — Them Bones
Alice in Chains — We Die Young
Alice in Chains — What the Hell Have I
Peabo Bryson — Can You Stop the Rain
>> Nick Cave w/ Kylie Minogue — Where the
    Wild Roses Grow
Nick Cave w/ P.J. Harvey — Henry Lee
Combustible Edison — Vertigogo
The Cramps — Bikini Girls with Machine Guns
The Cramps — Creature from the Black Leather
    Lagoon
Iris Dement — Our Town
Devo — Post Post Modern Man
Dramarama — Haven't Got a Clue
Gloria Estefan — It's Too Late
Gloria Estefan — You'll Be Mine (Party Time)
Faster Pussycat — Non Stop to Nowhere
Faster Pussycat — You're So Vain
Nanci Griffith — Speed of the Sound of Loneliness
Emmylou Harris — Thanks to You
Gladys Knight — Superwoman
Redd Kross — Annie's Gone
Redd Kross — Jimmy's Fantasy
Redd Kross — Lady in the Front Row
LA Guns — It's Over Now
LA Guns — Kiss My Love Goodbye
k.d. lang — Miss Chatelaine
Jerry Lee Lewis — Goosebumps
Martika — Coloured Kissed
Martini Ranch — How Does the Laboring Man
Meat Puppets — Backwater

Joni Mitchell — Come in from the Cold
Joni Mitchell — Night Ride Home
Joni Mitchell — Nothing Can Be Done
Joni Mitchell — Two Grey Rooms
Pearl Jam — Even Flow
Rancid — Pride
Sofia Shinas — One Last Kiss
>> Lisa Stansfield — Never Never Gonna Give You Up
Lisa Stansfield — The Line
Rod Stewart — If We Fall in Love Tonight
Van Halen — Fire in the Hole
Van Halen — Human Beings
Paul Westerberg — Love Untold
Chris Whitley — Livin' with the Law

JAKE SCOTT

Tori Amos — Past the Mission
Blind Melon — Galaxie
Tracy Bonham — Mother Mother
Bush — Comedown
Bush — Greedy Fly
The Cranberries — When You're Gone
Cypress Hill — Real Estate
Cypress Hill — Stoned Is the Way of the Walk
Digable Planets — Dial 7
Eels — Susan's House
Don Henley — Garden of Allah
John Lee Hooker — Mr. Lucky
k.d. lang — Hush Sweet Lover
k.d. lang — The Mind of Love
>> Live — Lightning Crashes
Live — Turn My Head
Natalie Merchant — Wonder
Ned's Atomic Dustbin — All I Ask of Myself Is That I >>
    Hold Together
No Doubt — New
Oasis — Morning Glory
Puff Daddy — Victory
Radiohead — Fake Plastic Trees
>> R.E.M — Everybody Hurts
The Rolling Stones — Out of Tears
Smashing Pumpkins — Disarm
Soundgarden — Burden in My Head
Soundgarden — Fell on Black Days
Spacehog — In the Meantime
Tina Turner — Golden Eye
>> U2 — Staring at the Sun
The Verve — On Your Own

STEPHANE SEDNAOUI

Fiona Apple — Sleep to Dream
>> Beck — Mixed Bizness
>> Björk — Big Time Sensuality
Björk — Possibly Maybe
The Black Crowes — Sometimes Salvation
Bush — Chemicals Between Us
Neneh Cherry and Youssou N'dour — Seven
    Seconds Away
Sheryl Crow — Sweet Child of Mine
Eram — Je Suis Mauvais
Eram — Les P'tits Clous
Eram — Passenger
Garbage — Milk

Garbage — Queer
Garbage — You Look So Fine
Go West — Shoes
Isaac Hayes — Fragile
Kula Shaker — Hey Dude
Traci Lords — Fallen Angel
M.C. Solaar — Le Nouveau Western
>> Madonna — Fever
Ziggy Marley — Kozmik
Massive Attack — Sly
Alanis Morissette — Ironic
Alanis Morissette — Thank U
NTM — Le Monde de Demain
NTM — Le Pouvoir
P.M. Dawn — Ways of the Wind
>> R.E.M. — Lotus
Red Hot Chili Peppers — Breaking the Girl
Red Hot Chili Peppers — Around the World
>> Red Hot Chili Peppers — Give It Away
Red Hot Chili Peppers — Scar Tissue
Smashing Pumpkins — Today
Tina Turner — Whatever You Want
Tricky — For Real
Tricky — Hell Is Round the Corner
Tricky — Pumpkin
U2 — Discotheque
U2 — Mysterious Ways

DOMINIC SENA

director,

video,

Bryan Adams — Victim of Love
Herb Albert — Our Song
Anita Baker — Talk to Me
Michael Bolton — Love Is a Wonderful Thing
>> Blue Nile — Headlights on the Parade
Toni Childs — Don't Walk Away
Robert Cray — Don't Be Afraid of the Dark
Taylor Dayne — I'll Be Your Shelter
Dream Academy — Indian Summer
Sheena Easton — The Lover in Me
Fleetwood Mac — As Long As You Follow
Janet Jackson — Come Back to Me
>> Janet Jackson — If
Janet Jackson — Let's Wait Awhile
Janet Jackson — Miss You Much
Janet Jackson — Pleasure Principle
Janet Jackson — Rhythm Nation
Richard Marx — Don't Mean Nothing
Richard Marx — Satisfied
Richard Marx — Should've Known Better
Maria McKee — Show Me Heaven
Robbie Neville — Who Needs Somebody Like You
Brenda Russell — Piano in the Dark
Sting — They Dance Alone
>> Tin Machine — One Shot
Tina Turner — I Don't Want to Lose You
John Waite — Restless Heart
Jody Watley — Don't You Want Me
Wendy & Lisa — Strung Out
Caron Wheeler — Blue Is the Color of Pain
Steve Winwood — One and Only
Pia Zadora — Heartbeat of Love

director.
video.

FLORIA SIGISMONDI

Barry Adamson — Can't Get Loose
David Bowie — Dead Man Walking
David Bowie — Little Wonder
Filter and the Crystal Method — Can You Trip
    Like I Do?
Fluffy — Black Eye
Ginger — Far Out
Harem Scarem — Blue
I Mother Earth — Not Quite Sonic
  » Marilyn Manson — The Beautiful People
  » Marilyn Manson — Tourniquet
Our Lady Peace — Birdman
Robert Plant and Jimmy Page — Most High
Pure — Anna Is a Speed Freak
Tea Party — Save Me
Tea Party — The River
Tea Party — The Search and Slant of Light
13 Engines — More
13 Engines — Smokin' Ashes
The Tony Rich Project — Nobody Knows
  » Tricky — Makes Me Wanna Die
Victory — Promise

director.
video.

WALTER STERN

Candyland — Bitter Moon
Candyland — Fountain of Youth
Candyland — Kingdom
Candyland — Rainbow
INXS — Elegantly Wasted
Loud — Easy
Madonna — Drowned World/Substitute for Love
Manic Street Preachers — Stay Beautiful
Marusha — Raveland
Massive Attack — Angel
Massive Attack — Risingson
Massive Attack — Teardrop
Moby — Hymn
  » Prodigy — Breathe
Prodigy — Firestarter
Prodigy — No Good
Prodigy — Poison
Prodigy — Voodoo People
The Spoons — Show Me How
Sweet Addiction — Enough Is Enough
Transister — Look Who's Perfect Now
  » The Verve — Bitter Sweet Symphony
World of Twist — Sweets

director.
video.

JOSH TAFT

Alice in Chains — Would
Asphalt Ballet — Tuesday's Rain
Kristen Barry — Let Me Be
Big Head Todd and the Monsters — Resignation
    Superman
Big Head Todd and the Monsters — In the Morning
Brand New Heavies — Dream on Dreamer
Counting Crows — Angels of the Silences
Cypress Hill — Insane in the Brain
De La Soul and Teenage Fanclub — Fallin'
Def Leppard — Tonight
Digable Planets — 19th Wonder

Fuel — Shimmer
Live — White Discussion
Manic Street Preachers — Scream to a Sigh
Meat Puppets — We Don't Exist
Midnight Oil — Truganini
Nas — The World Is Yours
Pearl Jam — Alive
Pearl Jam — Evenflow
  » Pearl Jam — Oceans
Adam Sandler — Lunchlady Land
Shaggy — Boom Bastic
Shaggy — Summertime
Slayer — I Hate You
Soundgarden — On the Skull
Stabbing Westward — What Do I Have to Do?
  » Stone Temple Pilots — Lady Picture Show
Stone Temple Pilots — Plush
Stone Temple Pilots — Sex Type Thing
Suicidal Tendencies — Alone
The Sundays — Wild Horses
311 — Down
Tribe Called Quest — Award Song
Tribe Called Quest — Electric Relaxation
Tribe Called Quest — Oh My God
Ugly Kid Joe — Milkman's Son
Ugly Kid Joe — Tomorrow's World
Paul Westerberg — Dyslexic Heart

TARSEM

  » Deep Forest — Sweet Lullaby
  » R.E.M. — Losing My Religion
Suzanne Vega — Tired of Sleeping

PAULA WALKER

Marc Anthony — I Need to Know
Baby Face — It's No Crime
Baby Face — Tender Love
Luka Bloom — Rescue Mission
  » Tracy Chapman — Talkin' About a Revolution
  » The Neville Brothers — Fearless
Tina Turner — Foreign Affair
Tina Turner — I Want You Near Me
Tina Turner — Look Me in the Heart
  » Tina Turner — Way of the World

HYPE WILLIAMS

Babyface — For the Lover in You
Blackstreet w/ Dr. Dre and Queen Pin — No Diggity
Blackstreet w/ Swv and Craig Mack — Tonight's the
    Night
Mary J. Blige — You Are My Everything
Mary J. Blige — Everything
Boyz II Men — Vybin
Brandy — Baby
Brandy — I Wanna Be Down
Brandy — Sitting in My Room
Brandy w/ Wanya of Boyz II Men — Broken Hearted
Bush — Jesus Online
D'Angelo — Lady
DMX, featuring Faith Evans — How's It Goin' Down?
    Finale

Dr. Dre and Tu-Pac — California Love
Jermaine Dupri and Mariah Carey — Sweetheart
Missy Elliot — The Rain (Supa Dupa Fly)
  » Missy Elliot — She's a Bitch
Missy Elliot, featuring Big Boi of Outkast and Nicole
    — All 'n' My Grill
Missy Elliot, featuring Da Brat and Li'l Kim — Sock It
    2 Me
Missy Elliot, featuring Nas, Lil' Mo, and Eve — Hot
    Boyz (remix)
Faith Evans — Love Like This
Jay-Z — Can't Knock the Hustle
Jay-Z, featuring Foxy Brown — Sunshine
K7 — Hi De Ho
Kelis — Caught Out There
R. Kelly — Down Low
R. Kelly — Gotham City
R. Kelly — Half on a Baby
R. Kelly — I Believe I Can Fly
R. Kelly — I Can't Sleep Baby (If I)
R. Kelly — Thank God It's Friday
R. Kelly, featuring Keith Murray — Home Alone
LL Cool J — Hey Lover
LL Cool J w/ Leshau — Doing It
LL Cool J w/ Total — Loungin'
Mase — Feels So Good
Mase, featuring Blackstreet — Get Ready
Method Man, featuring D'Angelo — Break Ups 2
    Make Ups
Mobb Deep, featuring Li'l Kim — Quiet Storm
Mya, featuring Noreaga and Raekwon — Movin' Out
Nas — Street Dreams
Nas w/ Lauryn Hill — If I Ruled the World
Nas, featuring Puff Daddy — Hate Me Now
Naughty By Nature — Craziest
No Doubt — My Ex-Girlfriend
Notorious B.I.G. — Big Poppa
Notorious B.I.G. — Warning
Ol' Dirty Bastard — Shimmy Shimmy Ya
Ol' Dirty Bastard — Got Cha Money
Kelly Price, featuring R. Kelly & Ron Isley — Friend
    of Mine
Puff Daddy and Faith Evans — Mo Money, Mo
    Problems
Puff Daddy, featuring R. Kelly — Satisfy You
Refugee Camp All Stars, featuring Pras and Ky-Mani
    — Avenues
Busta Rhymes — Dangerous (co-director: Busta
    Rhymes)
Busta Rhymes — Gimme Some Mo'
Busta Rhymes — Put Your Hands Where My Eyes
    Could See
Busta Rhymes — Woo Haa!! Got You All in Check
Busta Rhymes and Janet Jackson — What's It
    Gonna Be?
Scarface — Mary Jane
Will Smith — Gettin' Jiggy wit It
  » TLC — No Scrubs
Tribe Called Quest — Once Again and Stressed Out
Usher — The Many Ways
Usher — Nice and Slow
Usher — Think of You
Wu Tang Clan — Can It All Be Simple

WIZ

director.

video.

The Black Crowes — A Conspiracy
Brand New Heavies — Back to Love
Ian Brown — My Star
The Charlatans — Jesus Hairdo
>> The Chemical Brothers — Out of Control
DEE-Lite — Picnic in the Summertime
Del Amitri — Here and Now
DJ Rap — Bad Girl
Happy Mondays — Stinkin' Thinkin'
Jamiroquai — Emergency on Planet Earth
Manic Street Preachers — If You Tolerate This
Manic Street Preachers — Love's Sweet Exile
Manic Street Preachers — You Love Us
Marilyn Manson — Man That You Fear
>> Mel G. — Word Up
The Real People — The Truth
Simple Minds — Hypnotized
Suede — Drowners
Suede — He's Dead
Suede — Love and Poison
Suede — Metal Mikey
Suede — Moving
Suede — She's Not Dead
Therapy? — Diane
Therapy? — Loose

job#

CREDITS

director.

Akerlund, Jonas
Prodigy — Smack My Bitch Up
©1997 XL Recordings Ltd.

Madonna — Ray of Light
©1998 Warner Bros. Records, Inc.

Barish, Geoffrey
Spear of Destiny — Never Take Me Alive
©1987 Virgin Records America, Inc.
All Rights Reserved

John Hiatt — Have a Little Faith
©1987 A&M Records, Inc.

Lenny Kravitz — Mr. Cab Driver
©1990 Virgin Records America, Inc.
All Rights Reserved

Barron, Steve
a-ha — Take on Me
©1985 Warner Bros. Records, Inc.

Michael Jackson — Billie Jean
©1983 Sony Music Entertainment Inc.

Bayer, Samuel
Nirvana — Smells Like Teen Spirit
©1991 Geffen Records, Inc.

Smashing Pumpkins — Bullet With
Butterfly Wings
©1995 Virgin Records America, Inc.
All Rights Reserved

Garbage — Stupid Girl
©1996 Almo Sounds, Inc.

The Rolling Stones — Saint of Me
Copyright 1997 Promotone B.V.
All Rights Reserved

Sheryl Crow — Home
©1997 A&M Records, Inc.

Big TV!
The Wallflowers — Three Marlenas
©1997 Interscope Records

Lauryn Hill — Doo-Wop [That] Thing
©1998 Ruffhouse Records LP
Courtesy of Columbia Records

Blashfield, Jim
Talking Heads — And She Was
©1985 Sire Records Company

Joni Mitchell — Good Friends
©1985 Geffen Records, Inc.

Peter Gabriel — Don't Give Up
©1987 Geffen Records, Inc.

Bowden, Gavin
Live — Lakini's Juice
©1997 Radioactive Records, J.V.

Rage Against the Machine — No Shelter
©1998 Sony Music Entertainment Inc.

Red Hot Chili Peppers — Warped
©1995 Warner Bros. Records, Inc.

Boyd, Paul
Seal — A Prayer for the Dying
©1994 ZTT Records Ltd.
All Rights Reserved

Care, Peter
R.E.M. — Man on the Moon
©1992 R.E.M./Athens, Ltd.

R.E.M. — Drive
©1992 R.E.M./Athens, Ltd.

Tom Petty & the Heartbreakers — It's Good to
Be King
©1995 Warner Bros. Records, Inc.

R.E.M. — What's the Frequency, Kenneth?
©1994 R.E.M./Athens Ltd.

Corbijn, Anton
Nirvana — Heart Shaped Box
©1993 Geffen Records, Inc.

Rollins Band — Liar
©1994 Imago Recording Company

Cunningham, Chris
Squarepusher — Come on My Selector
©1997 Warp Records Limited

Aphex Twin — Come to Daddy
©1997 Warp Records Limited

Madonna — Frozen
©1998 Warner Bros. Records, Inc.

Portishead — Only You
©1997 Go! Beat Records

Björk — All Is Full of Love
©1999 Elektra Entertainment Group Inc.
©1999 One Little Indian Ltd.

Davis, Tamra
Luscious Jackson — City Song
©1994 Grand Royal/Capitol Records, Inc.

Sonic Youth — 100%
©1992 Geffen Records, Inc.

Veruca Salt — All Hail Me
©1995 Geffen Records, Inc.

Luscious Jackson — Ladyfingers
©1999 Grand Royal/Capitol Records, Inc.

Dayton/Faris
Smashing Pumpkins — Tonight, Tonight
©1996 Virgin Records America, Inc.
All Rights Reserved

Smashing Pumpkins — 1979
©1996 Virgin Records America, Inc.
All Rights Reserved

Porno for Pyros — Pets
©1993 Warner Bros. Records, Inc.

Neil Finn — She Will Have Her Way
©1998 Sony Music Entertainment, Inc.

Oasis — All Around the World
©1997 Sony Music Entertainment (UK) Ltd.

de Thame, Gerard
Black — Wonderful Life
©1987 A&M Records, Inc.

Tanita Tikaram — Cathedral Song
©1988 Warner Bros. Records, Inc.

Dick, Nigel
Oasis — Don't Go Away
©1997 Sony Music Entertainment (UK) Ltd.

Oasis — Wonderwall
©1996 Sony Music Entertainment (UK) Ltd.

Third Eye Blind — How's It Going to Be
©1997 Elektra Entertainment Group Inc.

Savage Garden — I Want You
©1997 Sony Music Entertainment Inc.

Matchbox 20 — Push
©1997 Atlantic Recording Group

Dom & Nic
David Bowie — I'm Afraid of Americans
©1997 Riskyfolio, Inc.

Dylan, Jesse
Nick Cave and the Bad Seeds —
Red Right Hand
©1994 Mute Records
All Rights Reserved

Tom Waits — Goin' Out West
©1992 Island Records Ltd.

Egan, Nick
Rancid — Bloodclot
©1998 Epitaph, A California Corporation

Manbreak — Ready or Not
©1997 One Little Indian Records
All Rights Reserved

Alanis Morissette — You Oughta Know
©1995 Maverick Recording Company

Fincher, David
George Michael — Freedom 90
©1990 CBS Records (UK) Ltd.

Iggy Pop — Home
©1990 Virgin Records America, Inc.
All Rights Reserved

The Rolling Stones — Love Is Strong
©1994 Virgin BENELUX, B.V.

Madonna — Vogue
©1990 Sire Records Company

Madonna — Express Yourself
©1989 Sire Records Company

Billy Idol — Cradle of Love
©1990 Virgin Records America, Inc.
All Rights Reserved

Glazer, Jonathan
Radiohead — Karma Police
©1997 EMI Records Ltd.(worldwide)
Radiohead Appears Courtesy of Parlophone

Jamiroquai — Virtual Insanity
©1996 Sony Music Entertainment (UK) Ltd.

Radiohead — Street Spirit (Fade Out)
©1996 EMI Records Ltd. (worldwide)
Radiohead Appears Courtesy of Parlophone

Godley, Kevin & Lol Creme
Herbie Hancock — Rock-it
©1984 CBS Video Enterprises

Forest for the Trees — Dream
©1997 SKG Music LLC

U2 — The Sweetest Thing
©1998 Polygram Int. Music BV

The Charlatans — Forever
©1999 Universal/Island Records Ltd.

The Police — Every Breath You Take
©1983 A&M Records Limited

Gondry, Michel
Beck — Deadweight
©1997 A&M Records Inc.

Björk — Human Behavior
©1993 Elektra Entertainment Group Inc.
©1993 One Little Indian Ltd.

Cibo Matto — Sugar Water
©1996 Warner Bros. Records Inc.

Foo Fighters — Everlong
©1997 Roswell Records/Capitol Records, Inc.

The Rolling Stones — Like a Rolling Stone
©1995 Virgin Records Ltd.
All Rights Reserved

Greenhalgh, Howard
Soundgarden — Black Hole Sun
©1994 A&M Records, Inc.

Counting Crows — Daylight Fading
©1997 Geffen Records, Inc.

Placebo — Bruise Pristine
©1997 Virgin Records Ltd.
All Rights Reserved

Greif, Paula & Peter Kagan
Iggy Pop — Wild America
©1993 Virgin Records America, Inc.
All Rights Reserved

Duran Duran — Skin Trade
©1987 EMI Records

Cutting Crew — [I Just] Died in Your Arms
Version #2
©1986 Virgin Records America, Inc.

Haussman, Michael
Madonna — Take a Bow
©1994 Sire Records Company

Hogan, David
Sheryl Crow — Leaving Las Vegas
©1994 A&M Records Inc.

Shania Twain — You're Still the One
©1997 Mercury Records

Steve Miller Band — Ya Ya
©1988 Capitol Records, Inc.

Hunter, Paul
Erykah Badu — On and On
©1996 Universal Records

LL Cool J — Phenomenon
©1997 Def Jam Records, Inc.

Marilyn Manson — Dope Show
©1998 Nothing Records

0:02:68

Lenny Kravitz — American Woman
©1999 Virgin Records America, Inc.
All Rights Reserved

Lenny Kravitz — Fly Away
©1998 Virgin Records America, Inc.
All Rights Reserved

>> **Joanou, Phil**
Tom Petty & the Heartbreakers — Walls
©1996 Warner Bros. Records, Inc.

U2 — One (version 2)
©1992 Not Us Ltd.

U2 — Wild Horses
©1992 Not Us Ltd.

>> **Jonze, Spike**
Notorious B.I.G. — Sky's the Limit
©1997 Bad Boy Entertainment

Björk — It's Oh So Quiet
©1995 Elektra Entertainment Group Inc.
©1995 One Little Indian Ltd.

Wax — California
©1995 Interscope Records

Beastie Boys — Sabotage
©1994 Capitol Records, Inc.

M.C. 900 Foot Jesus — If I Only Had a Brain
©1994 American Recordings

>> **Karr, Dean**
Dave Matthews Band — Don't Drink the Water
©1998 BMG Entertainment

Dave Matthews Band — Crash Into Me
©1996 BMG Entertainment

Marilyn Manson — Sweet Dreams Are Made of This
©1995 Nothing/Interscope Records

>> **Kerslake, Kevin**
Red Hot Chili Peppers — Soul to Squeeze
©1993 Warner Bros. Records Inc.

Mazzy Star — Fade into You
©1994 Capitol Records Inc.

Nirvana — In Bloom
©1992 Geffen Records, Inc.

R.E.M. — Sidewinder Sleeps Tonite
©1992 R.E.M./Athens, Ltd.

Stone Temple Pilots — Vasoline
©1994 Atlantic Recording Corporation

Nirvana — Come As You Are
©1992 Geffen Records, Inc.

Stone Temple Pilots — Interstate Love Song
©1994 Atlantic Recording Corporation

Sam Phillips — I Need Love
©1994 Virgin Records America, Inc.
All Rights Reserved

>> **Lambert, Mary**
Madonna — Like a Prayer
©1989 Sire Records Company

>> **Lawrence, Francis**
Ginuwine — What's So Different
©1999 Sony Music Entertainment Inc.

Seal — Human Beings
©1998 Warner Bros. Records, Inc.

Maxwell — Fortunate
©Rock Land Records/Interscope Records

>> **Libman, Leslie & Larry Williams**
Iggy Pop — Living on the Edge of the Night
©1989 Paramount Pictures and Virgin Records America, Inc.
All Rights Reserved

Bee Gees — You Win Again
©1987 Warner Bros. Records, Inc.

Belinda Carlisle — Mad About You
©1986 I.R.S. Records, Inc.

>> **Mahurin, Matt**
Bush — Little Things
©1995 Interscope Records

Hole — Gold Dust Woman
©1996 Hollywood Records

>> **Maybury, John (i)**
Sinead O'Connor — Nothing Compares 2 U
©1990 Ensign Records Ltd.

Shara Nelson — Down that Road
©1994 Chrysalis Records

>> **McDaniel, Melodie**
Madonna — Secret
©1994 Sire Records Company

Patti Smith — Don't Smoke in Bed
©1995 Good Karma, Inc.
Courtesy of Arista Records, Inc.

Porno for Pyros — Cursed Female
©1993 Warner Bros. Records, Inc.

>> **McFarlane, Keir**
Tom Petty & The Heartbreakers — Mary Jane's Last Dance
©1993 MCA Records Inc.

Candlebox — Simple Lessons
©1995 Maverick Recording Company

>> **Mondino, Jean-Baptiste**
Madonna — Justify My Love
©1990 Sire Records Company

Madonna — Human Nature
©1995 Boy Toy Records

Don Henley — Boys of Summer
©1984 Geffen Records, Inc.

Me'Shell Ndegéocello — If That's Your Boyfriend [He Wasn't Last Night]
©1994 Maverick Recording Company

>> **Muller, Sophie**
Annie Lennox — Why
©1992 BMG Records (UK) LTD
All Rights Reserved

Björk — Venus as a Boy
©1993 Elektra Entertainment Group Inc.
©1993 One Little Indian Ltd.

>> **Nichol, Doug**
Aerosmith — Pink
©1997 Sony Music Entertainment Inc.
Courtesy of Aerosmith and Aerodisc Partnership

Pulp — This Is Hardcore
©1998 Island Records Ltd.

>> **Nispel, Marcus**
No Doubt — Spiderwebs
©1995 Interscope Records

Puff Daddy — Victory
©1997 Bad Boy Entertainment

Fugees — Ready or Not
©1996 Sony Music Entertainment Inc.

Bush — Greedy Fly
©1996 Interscope Records

>> **Pellington, Mark**
Pearl Jam — Jeremy
©1992 Epic Records Inc.

U2 — One (buffalo version)
©1992 Not Us Ltd.

Nine Inch Nails — We're in this Together
©1999 Nothing Records, Inc.

>> **Plansker, Jeffrey**
10,000 Maniacs — Candy Everybody Wants
©1992 Elektra Entertainment Group Inc.

Robbie Robertson — Mahk Jchi
©1994 Capitol Records Inc.

Urge Overkill — Positive Bleeding
©1993 Geffen Records, Inc.

Soundgarden — Spoonman
©1994 A&M Records, Inc.

>> **Pope, Tim**
The Cure — The Lovecats
©1982 Fiction Records Ltd.
Reproduced with kind permission

>> **Proyas, Alex**
INXS — Kiss the Dirt [Falling Down the Mountain]
©1986 Atlantic Recording Corp. and INXS

Sting — All This Time
©1991 A&M Records Inc.

>> **Ritts, Herb**
Chris Isaak — Wicked Game
©1991 Reprise Records

Madonna — Cherish
©1989 Sire Records Company

Janet Jackson — Love Will Never Do without You
©1990 A&M Records Inc.

>> **Rolston, Matthew**
Jewel — Foolish Games
©1997 Atlantic Recording Corporation

Marilyn Manson — Long Hard Road out of Hell
©1997 Sony Music Entertainment Inc.

Garbage — I Think I'm Paranoid
©1998 Almo Sounds, Inc.

Lenny Kravitz — Thinking of You
©1998 Virgin Records America, Inc.
All Rights Reserved

>> **Romanek, Mark**
Beck — Devil's Haircut
©1996 Geffen Records, Inc.

Fiona Apple — Criminal
©1997 Work Group/Clean Slate

Lenny Kravitz — If You Can't Say No
©1998 Virgin Records America, Inc.

Madonna — Bedtime Stories
©1995 and Courtesy Boy Toy, Inc. and Maverick Recording Company/Warner Bros. Records

Nine Inch Nails — Closer
©1994 Nothing/TVT/Interscope

Nine Inch Nails — Perfect Drug
©1997 Nothing/TVT/Interscope

>> **Schenk, Rocky**
Nick Cave & Kylie Minogue — Where the Wild Roses Grow
©1995 Mute Records
All Rights Reserved

Lisa Stansfield — Never Never Gonna Give You Up
©1997 BMG Eurodisc Limited
Courtesy of Arista Records, Inc.
All Rights Reserved

>> **Scott, Jake**
Live — Lightning Crashes
©1995 Radioactive Records J.V.

U2 — Staring at the Sun
©1997 U2 Limited

R.E.M. — Everybody Hurts
©1993 R.E.M./Athens, Ltd.

>> **Sednaoui, Stephane**
Björk — Big Time Sensuality
©1993 Elektra Entertainment Group Inc.
©1993 One Little Indian Ltd.

Red Hot Chili Peppers — Give It Away
©1991 Warner Bros. Records, Inc.

Madonna — Fever
©1993 Sire Records Company

R.E.M. — Lotus
©1998 R.E.M./Athens LLC

Beck — Mixed Bizness
©2000 Geffen Records, Inc.

>> **Sena, Dominic**
Janet Jackson — If
©1993 Virgin Records America Inc.

Blue Nile — Headlights on the Parade
©1990 A&M Records Inc.

Tin Machine — One Shot
©1989, 1997 Jones/Tintoretto Entertainment Co., LLC

>> **Sigismondi, Floria**
Marilyn Manson — Tourniquet
©1997 Nothing Records

Marilyn Manson — The Beautiful People
©1996 Nothing/Interscope

Tricky — Makes Me Wanna Die
©1997 Island Records Ltd.

>> **Stern, Walter**
The Verve — Bitter Sweet Symphony
©1997 Virgin Records Ltd.
©1997 Hut Recordings

Prodigy — Breathe
©1997 XL Recordings Ltd.

>> **Taft, Josh**
Stone Temple Pilots — Lady Picture Show
©1996 Atlantic Recording Corporation

Pearl Jam — Oceans
©1991 Sony Music Entertainment Inc.

>> **Tarsem**
Deep Forest — Sweet Lullaby
©1993 Sony Music Entertainment Inc.

R.E.M. — Losing My Religion
©1991 Warner Bros. Records, Inc.

>> **Walker, Paula**
Tracy Chapman — Talkin' Bout a Revolution
©1989 Elektra Entertainment Group Inc.

Tina Turner — Way of the World
©1991 Capitol Records, Inc.

The Neville Brothers — Fearless
©1990 A&M Records Inc.

>> **Williams, Hype**
TLC — No Scrubs
©1999 La Face Records

Missy Elliot — She's a Bitch
©1999 Elektra Entertainment Group Inc.

>> **Wiz**
Mel G. — Word Up
©1999 Virgin Records America, Inc.
All Rights Reserved

The Chemical Bros. — Out of Control
©1999 Virgin Records America, Inc.
All Rights Reserved

job#

Page numbers in *italics* refer to illustrations.

director:

BIOGRAPHIES

SPIKE JONZE: M.C. 900 FT. JESUS   IF I ONLY HAD A BRAIN
1994   >>

(NEIL FEINEMAN)

S.R.

>> Fifteen years ago **Steve Reiss** was running a public access station in Del Mar, California, and shooting underground bands, surf culture, and performance artists. Drawn to music video's experimental, inventive nature, he landed a freelance post-production position with Propaganda Films, specializing in visual effects. Since then he has worked on projects with a variety of artists such as Michael Jackson, Lenny Kravitz, Madonna, U2, David Bowie, and Alanis Morissette. He was producer on the Breeders' "Cannonball" video for Spike Jonze, associate producer on the *R.E.M. Road Movie* for Peter Care, and co-producer on Lauryn Hill's "Everything is Everything" for Sanji. He has also worked with Satellite Films, Palomar, Partizan, and Little Minx on music videos, commercials, and special venue and new media ventures, and he packaged *Mark Romanek — Music Video Stills* (Tondo). Reiss lives in Venice, California.

N.F.

>> **Neil Feineman** has covered the music and video scene for twenty years for publications such as the *L.A. Weekly*, the *Los Angeles Times, Trouser Press,* and *The Face.* He was the founding editor of award-winning magazines such as *RayGun, Beach Culture,* and *Gravity,* which all investigated the world of sound in film as well as popular culture. He has written several books on popular culture and is the editor-in-chief of the new music magazine, *Revolution.* Feineman lives in San Francisco.

T.D.

>> While dying shoes in a women's shoe store at age 15, **Steve Tolleson** knew he was taking a "step" in the right direction. Today, he is principal of Tolleson Design based in San Francisco. In business for over 16 years, the studio now consists of 14 people who believe in playing every bit as hard as they work. Steve's approach to graphic design has garnered him recognition throughout a multitude of industries including music/entertainment, retail, publishing, technology, and — most recently — motion graphics. His client base encompasses a diverse range from Virgin Interactive to Nike, Urban Outfitters, Netscape, Verve Records, Liz Claiborne, Disney, and The San Francisco Ballet, among others. The studio's work and ideology was recently captured in a book published by Princeton Architectural Press titled *soak wash rinse spin.*

edit 1.

edit 3.